# THE

# Journey

## WE MUST ALL TAKE

# THE
# *Journey*
## WE MUST ALL TAKE

The Credibility, the Prominence,
the Way of Christianity

## AL PEREZ

# THE JOURNEY WE MUST ALL TAKE
# THE CREDIBILITY, THE PROMINENCE,
# THE WAY OF CHRISTIANITY

iUniverse books may be ordered through booksellers or by contacting:

iUniverse
1663 Liberty Drive
Bloomington, IN 47403
www.iuniverse.com
1-800-Authors (1-800-288-4677)

ISBN: 978-1-4917-5147-3 (sc)
ISBN: 978-1-4917-5148-0 (e)

Library of Congress Control Number: 2014919446

Printed in the United States of America.

iUniverse rev. date: 11/12/2014

To my mom, dad, wife, four sons,
and five grandchildren—

Julius,
Colden,
Rowan,
Connor, and
Leighton—
*my inspiration.*

# Contents

# The Journey Begins

Everything has a beginning, and although the beginning of our journey may be quite innocuous, it soon changes.

> The Journey starts almost instantly after fertilization. The egg splits, then splits again, and then unnoticeably, quietly, and compassionately, He appears, hovers over the rapidly multiplying egg transforming into an embryo, smiles lovingly at it, and gently breathes life into this little miracle. So it begins, the journey that will take this breath, which is now a soul, a soul within its growing temporal body, into eternity.

The belief that life is sacred and the soul is eternal is central to Christianity, which according to many in our current culture is just one of many religions. But is it? What is Christianity? How does it differ from other major world belief systems? Do they really differ? Or do all religions eventually lead to the same mountaintop? Common sense makes it very difficult to believe that opposing views could all be right.

Is there one true religion? If there is, it is certainly prudent that we know which is the true one because regardless of who we are or what we believe, each of us is on the segment of our journey we call life. This earthly life will end. Then what?

*Always be prepared to give an answer to everyone who*
*asks you to give the reason for the hope that you have.*
—1 Peter 3:15

# Preface

Several years back, one cool, crisp, country morning, I was sipping coffee and watching the first rays of the sun break through the treetops. It started as a gnawing feeling in the pit of my stomach; the feeling grew and exploded into the realization I was approaching retirement age. What had happened to the years?

As my mind wandered, I began to recall the seminal events in my life. Having been raised in a Christian home, at seventeen, I left Texas and entered college in California. I enlisted in the air force, where I finished college through graduate school. I started a family, earned an officer's commission, went to war in Vietnam, became a commercial pilot, taught Park College undergraduate courses and Golden Gate University graduate business law, and became a practicing CPA.

Now that I've retired, it has been hard for me to rationalize the many blessings my family—now consisting of a wife, four sons, and five grandchildren—and I have received. Among all the material goods and personal and family accomplishments, there was still a sense of incompleteness. This empty sense began to draw me back to Christianity. For many years, my wife, a "cradle" Catholic, had wanted to get remarried in the Catholic Church. A dear friend, the late Monico Cisneros, sponsored me through the year-long Roman Catholic Indoctrination for Adults (RCIA) class. We subsequently did remarry in the church.

This experience was but a starting point. It was the beginning of a ten-year and ongoing exploration and study of the Bible, Christianity, and various major religions.

The exploratory phase of my studies included many discussions with theologians, lay pastors, and many regular, everyday folks, some of whom attended church regularly and a few who had never darkened the threshold of any church. A significant portion of this book, part 1, provides lay answers to questions raised by these folks.

So what is this book about? It is basically an apologetics book that compares Christianity to the other major world belief systems. Most of the comparison is from a secular, lay perspective. The objective is to provide useful information that will help us get through this journey we call life and into that which awaits us.

# Acknowledgments

I thank the many people who helped me put this effort together, including my sons and friends who contributed the questions addressed in the first part of this book, and my wife, Wilma, whose experience as a schoolteacher was invaluable in bringing this effort to fruition. Special thanks to Harry Koch, a personal friend and family member, who spent countless hours proofreading and helping with corrections.

# Introduction

Humanity has always been inquisitive; in its constant search for knowledge, human beings have unraveled many mysteries and have made much progress in the search for answers. Yet to this day, most of us have struggled to obtain satisfactory answers to some questions.

- Where did I come from?
- What am I doing here?
- What will happen to me after I die?

How do we go about finding answers to these questions? Some look to science, others to philosophy, and still others to other disciplines, yet throughout history, people have most often looked to some form of religion for answers because nothing else has provided reasonable answers and because we are driven to believe in something or someone outside ourselves. If this need is denied, we experience a void, an incompleteness. Even hard-core atheists who claim they are complete unto themselves have to work to try to convince themselves, but if they are honest, they will not succeed. The various religions represent our attempts to fill this void.

This presents its own problem. There are so many religions in the world; most claim to be the only true religion and that all others are pretenders, cults, or just plain false religions. So are they all right, or is there only one true religion? This is the core question we will try to answer.

To initiate the exploratory phase of our journey, we will address a few interesting questions concerning religion. We will then look at some tools that will help us review the major religions. Our journey will then move on to a review of these belief systems with short analyses. We will conclude with a more in-depth review of Christianity.

All biblical references (unless specifically indicated otherwise) in this book are to the New International Version (NIV) of the Bible.

## Part 1:

# Answering the Questions

# Chapter 1

I thanked my daughter-in-law for the great meal my wife and I had just shared with my oldest son and his family. After some small talk, my son asked if I would be interested in going for a short walk to burn off calories and perhaps stop at a coffee shop for a cup of coffee.

As we walked and visited, I guided the conversation toward church and religion. After some overly general discussion on various religious topics, we stopped. I looked at my son and asked him if he believed in God. He thought for a moment and rather hesitantly answered yes, he did, but there were so many different beliefs, so many different churches, and so many different religions out there that he wasn't sure which one was the right one. How could any religion claim to be the only valid one when everybody had what they considered to be the real truth?

# There Are So Many Religions; How Can We Know Which One if Any Is the True Religion?

To answer this question, it will be necessary to understand the following three concepts. The first concept, worldviews, will help us understand why different people often arrive at different conclusions when observing or analyzing the same information. This occurs because everyone interprets data received by their senses through a filter, his or her worldview, which is based on presuppositions, which in turn are based on truth claims. The following examples should help us better understand what truth claims are.

I remember an aging male fifth-grade schoolteacher explaining to the class that men with receding hairlines were naturally smarter than those with full heads of hair; that was a truth claim. A next-door neighbor, a highly successful businessperson, said he would never hire young women in responsible positions because they were too high maintenance; that was a truth claim. An ardent pro-abortionist believes a three-month-old fetus is not a life; another truth claim.

The validity of any worldview is entirely determined by the validity of the truth claim(s) on which it is based. Once we understand the truth claims, we can establish the appropriateness of the worldview if we have an objective understanding of truth.

The second concept we need to get a handle on is to get a clear understanding of truth: What is truth? How can anyone claim to know the truth when there are so many differing viewpoints?

Most people probably believe that defining truth is a difficult proposition. However, to understand and define truth, we must move beyond political correctness and go back to the basics: truth is what is real; it is the way things are regardless of what we think or what we want them to be. This concept is what is known as the correspondence theory of truth. To more directly paraphrase this concept, if it is real, it is true, and if it is not real, it is not true. There is no equivocation to this concept; it is or it is not.

I must point out that absolute truth is rare; the overwhelming number of decisions we make every day are based on the probability the information we are relying on is true.

For the third concept, we will take a look at two laws of logic. These principles will help us deal with the following argument. Muslims, Mormons, and Christians (among others) claim that their respective religions are the one true religion. Could they all be right?

Of the various principles of logic, we will concentrate on the two that most directly assist us in addressing the above argument.

The first one is the law of noncontradiction, which states that something cannot be two different things at the same time and in the same sense. If contradictions could exist at the same time and in the same sense, black could be white and up would be no different from down.

The second one is the law of inference, which states that if you can verify the truthfulness of your premise, you can derive logical and/or true conclusions. You do not have to verify the truthfulness of the conclusion, just its premise. In the following example, you can easily identify the premises and should be able to undoubtedly accept their truthfulness. That being true, the truthfulness of the conclusion is unquestionable. Example: "All humans are mortal. I am a human. Therefore, I am mortal."

Let us then address the question, "There are so many religions; how can we know which one if any is the true religion?" I won't spend too much time addressing atheism because the question is concerned with which religion is the true religion, not that there is no religion. The one exception to atheism not being a religion is secular humanism, which claims to be a religion that doesn't believe there is a God but that humanity is the ultimate supreme being.

So now we have an atheistic religion that believes humanity is the supreme being, religions such as Hinduism that believe in many gods or that everything is God, and religions that believe there is only one God, such as Islam, Judaism, and Christianity. The law of noncontradiction tells us all these claims cannot be true. They could all be false, but no more than one can be true. So how can we determine which one is true?

If you tend toward the supremacy of humanity, you believe there is nothing past the material, that nature, hence natural law, accounts for everything. But natural law cannot explain the creation of matter or its transformation into living, breathing beings. Absent any outside force, nature tends toward disorder, so natural law cannot explain the orderliness of the universe. Again, absent any outside force, nature tends toward decay while evolution requires continual improvement; natural law cannot account for this disparity. Natural law states that everything that exists has a cause, but matter exists, so what caused it? Natural law cannot explain its causality. The list goes on and on. All of these phenomena cannot be accounted for by natural law; since they did occur, they must have occurred outside natural law, in other words, supernaturally. Atheists deny the supernatural; hence, they deny themselves. This conclusion is supported by the natural law of logic, the law of inference.

If you tend toward the belief that everything is God, things get really murky. Of all the religions that believe in multiple gods or that everything is God, only Hinduism has a significant historical record in the Vedas, a collection of hymns, prayers, and some liturgical formulas believed to have been written around 700–800 BC. Otherwise, most of these religions are a potpourri of ideas and beliefs with relatively short histories and limited written contemporary records. The worldviews on which these religions depend are themselves difficult to assess because their truth claims are unverifiable; they must be taken strictly and completely on faith.

If you tend toward the belief that there is only one God, you are in the company of Muslims, Jews, and Christians. In 2005, Christians accounted for 33 percent of the world's population, while Muslims accounted for 21 percent. These two belief systems represent the majority of the people in the world.

Jews and Christians have a written history dating to approximately 1250 BC. The Muslim religion started some 1,800 years later, about AD 620. The Muslims have the Qur'an as their primary religious guide, while Jews and Christians have the Bible. The Hebrew Bible is for all accounts and purposes the same as the Christian Old Testament.

The Qur'an is based on information received by Muhammad over approximately twenty years, while the Bible was written by some forty men over approximately 1,400 years. Information in the Bible has been proven to such a degree that almost all its truth claims have been shown to be true. Those truth claims that have not been proven are those outside the realm of scientific scrutiny. The logical law of inference has given a great degree of credibility to these truth claims.

Postmodernism (PM) is a relatively new phenomenon (within the past forty to fifty years) that deserves our attention. This rapidly expanding belief system has taken the Western world by storm. PM rejects people's ability to reason their way to truth. The reason is simple—postmodernists believe there is no truth. According to PM, truth is subjective and comes from human ideas and experience interpreted through our culture. In other words, truth is relative.

Our political correctness, the blurring of the lines between right and wrong, the degradation of the sanctity of marriage, and a similar degradation of the sanctity of life itself, demands for complete tolerance for their belief system but not for opposing beliefs. Other similar and recent social changes were for the most part initiated by secular humanists and were accepted and heartily championed by postmodernists. Whether this belief system is a religion or not is still open to interpretation; it is probably more a lifestyle than a religion. However you classify it, it is certainly a force to be reckoned with.

So in answering my son's question and carefully using only natural law and reasoning while refraining from using any spiritual thought processes requiring faith outside the natural, I believe I have provided sufficient information to help you decide which religion you believe is the true one. I believe the secular evidence overwhelmingly supports the Christian claim of being the one true religion.

# Chapter 2

**Lockhart, Texas, November 2009**

Calmly, in military uniform, Major Nidal Hasan entered the U.S Army military post's outprocessing center, unholstered his weapon, and loudly proclaimed, "Allahu Akbar" ("Allah is great") and started shooting. Ten minutes later, thirteen soldiers lay dead and twenty-nine were wounded.

Shortly after the terrorist attack, a few friends and I were watching a news channel that featured a panel of experts discussing the attack. After the usual pointing of fingers and attempts at assessing fault, one of the panelists asked, "Why all the terrorist attacks? Are they really doing it because that is what Allah wants them to do?" Another panelist said he wasn't sure but that up until recently, he had always thought that the Allah of the Muslims and the God of the Christian Bible were one and the same. Of course, this confused the issue even more. Shortly thereafter, and without the panel reaching any conclusive position, the program signed off.

We sat silently for a few minutes. One of my friends looked at me and said, "You're a churchgoing person, what do you think? Is the God of Christianity and the Allah of Islam the same God?" Prior to his question, I had been trying to come to grips with the panelist's question. Hesitatingly, I stammered that I hoped not. I had not given the issue much thought, so I resolved to try to find out.

# Is the Allah of Islam and the God of the Bible One and the Same?

In Arabic, the word for god is *Allah*. Before Muhammad started his new religion, most Arabs worshipped 360 gods, one for each day of the lunar year. Many Arab families would choose a favorite god. Muhammad's favorite god was Allah, the moon god.

While he was growing up, the tribe he belonged to was constantly at war, so it was probably out of necessity that he became a very good warrior. Muhammad would often seek solitude, so while alone in one of his village's nearby caves, an angel appeared to him and started a series of visits and revelations that lasted some twenty years. Since he was unable to read or write, he passed the revelations to his friends who later wrote them down, and they formed the Qur'an.

As Muhammad received his revelations, he began to start his new religion; he of course chose his favorite god, Allah, as the only Islamic God. In addition to using persuasion and discourse to acquire converts, Muhammad claimed that Allah commanded him to fight people until they became Muslims.

By the time Muhammad died in AD 632, he had converted many Arabs to his new religion; much of the conversion was done at the point of the sword.

Similarities between the Muslim and Christian views of God exist. Christians and Muslims believe in one eternal God who created the universe, and both believe God is all-powerful, all-knowing, and all-present. To a Muslim, Allah is the only God, and all other gods are false. The Bible tells Christians there are many would-be gods but there is only one true God—all others are false.

There the similarities end. The God of the Bible rejects all attempts to forcefully convert anyone. All conversions must be completely willful and with knowledge and understanding. Anyone who is "converted" under duress is actually not converted at all.

Christianity is a religion of love, love of God and love of neighbor. Islam? Not so much.

So no, the concept that Muslims have of Allah precludes any possibility that the Allah of Islam and the God of the Bible are the same. Muslims say that the entire Christian Bible, with the exception of the first five books in the Old Testament and portions of the gospel, is corrupted and without merit. Since the Bible is the Word of God and since Christianity relies completely on the Bible, if you reject the Bible, you reject God. So Muslims themselves exclude the possibility that Allah and the God of the Bible are the same.

I'll offer more-detailed information on this in part 3.

# Chapter 3

**San Antonio, Texas, April 2004**

On a beautiful April afternoon, an old air force friend and I were sitting in his backyard reminiscing. Our friendship went back to the late 1970s, when we were both stationed at Luke Air Force Base in Arizona.

Comfortable with each other's company, we discussed many topics, from our past military exploits to what we had been involved in recently. Knowing that he was attending a Catholic church with his wife, we started talking about religion. After telling him I had recently completed the RCIA course, I asked him what he thought about the Bible.

He thought for a long moment, looked me in the eye, and said he believed the Bible was a "good" book. It had a lot of good guidance and many good stories. Noticing his hesitation, I said, "It's a good book, but?"

He said that even though it was a good book, it was impossible to believe everything in it. How could a man live for three days in the belly of a fish? Impossible!

Walking on water, destroying every living thing by drowning, coming back from the dead? No, he said, the Bible was a good book, but there was a lot of myth and, for lack of a better word, fiction in it.

Believing that his resoluteness would respond only to reasoning based on secular argument, I responded rather unconvincingly that although I believed the Bible was true, I could understand his position.

I determined to study the history of the Bible.

11

# What Proof Do We Have That the Bible Is True? Or Is It Myth and Fiction?

If the Bible can be shown to be a fictional book, a mythical book, a book based on fantasy or a book based on even half-truths, the Christianity established by the apostles and early church fathers with guidance provided by the Creator himself would cease to exist. Without the Bible, there would be no followers of Christ, no Christians, and no Christianity.

A few things the Bible is not. It is not a book whose contents were revealed to one man, as were the Qur'an and the Book of Mormon. Nor was it written by the same man as was the Book of Mormon. No, the Bible was written by some forty authors who, on the whole, lived and experienced that which they wrote about.

Examples of these authors include Joshua, who lived through the forty-year exodus from Egypt and led the conquering of the promised land, and the prophet Samuel, who lived through the era of the judges and the first two Israelite kings. Additional authors include the second and third Israelite kings, King David, and King Solomon. Examples of New Testament authors include the apostles Matthew, John, Peter, Paul, and others. No, the Bible was written over a fourteen-hundred-year period by men who were inspired by God, who were there, and who for the most part lived it.

Although written by many men over a long period, the Bible reads as if it were written by one person; this can be explained only by its divinely inspired nature. As to its truthfulness, the Bible has undergone scrutiny for over two thousand years. The standards by which the Bible has been tested have run the gamut. Every time a discovery is made that seems to contradict the Bible, much fanfare is always made. But these "contradictions" almost always are about a group of people referenced in the Bible, such as the Hittites, or a biblical city, or a distinguished personage, who apparently did not exist. Invariably, further research always supports the Bible. When such claims are refuted, the news releases if any are always muted. These tests have been so thorough and convincing that it can be safely stated without equivocation that no archaeological discovery has ever been proven to controvert the Bible.

Let us expand on biblical inspiration. During the Middle Ages, when the black plague tore through Europe and killed millions, many blamed the plague on the Jews. All different groups of people from every walk of life were dying in huge numbers except the Jews. Since the Jews weren't dying, they were obviously the ones who had started it, in the thinking of many.

The reason for this was that some two thousand years earlier, after the Ten Commandments were given to Moses, with inspired guidance, he wrote very specific instructions to guide daily Jewish life that became known as the Mosaic Law. These included the washing of hands before eating, building bathrooms outside living areas, quarantining people with various illnesses, and among others, specific guidance when dealing with the dead. These rules very obviously served them well during the black plague. Did those of Moses' time know about bacteriological threats? It is prudent to say they did not. Inspired? The Bible abounds with other examples of specific information the authors could not have understood.

Continuing with the inspired nature of the Bible, we will look at prophesy, the foretelling of the future not in general terms but in specific terms. The writer of a prophesy would have no foreknowledge or any ability to foresee the future. Biblical scholars have itemized some 780 major individual prophesies (some figures range as high as nearly 1,500, but many of these are rather minor or have already been prophesized by one or more authors) in the Bible, of which over 325 concern the birth, life, death, and resurrection of Jesus, the Messiah.

A survey of these prophecies shows that all that have had to do with events or circumstances up to the present have, in fact, occurred—as prophesized. Those that have not occurred normally concern the Second Coming of Christ. The discipline of statistics does not have a numerical figure large enough to enumerate the possibility that all of these prophecies could have occurred by chance.

Okay, so we know that the Bible, for the most part, was written by men who lived what they wrote about, who were inspired to write things they often could not possibly have understood or had any foreknowledge of, and whose prophecies for the most part have come true. So how can we know that what they originally wrote is in fact what we have in our current translations of the Bible?

It is true that all the original writings no longer exist (a fragment of the apostle John's writing does exist, but it is a very small fragment). It is, however, a good thing that the originals no longer exist. If you wanted to preserve the authenticity of an original, old, and valuable writing, how would you do it? You would have the original written on relatively short-lived material such as papyrus or other degradable material. You would have continual copies of these writings made and spread throughout the world. Instead of one original, you would then have hundreds of thousands of copies of the original. As hundreds of years go by, you can draw on the copies of copies throughout the world to compare authenticity. This is exactly what happened. The fidelity these copies have to one another has been amazing. Did all of this happen by accident? I think not.

If the original had been preserved, it would have been owned and controlled by people. Suspicions would no doubt abound—Did they somehow alter the original? Can we trust the original? These suspicions are not a problem when thousands upon thousands of copies exist, and the number grows; the Bible is still the best-selling book. All of these copies are easy to compare to each other.

So we now have archaeological evidence of the truthfulness of the Bible, and we have historical evidence of the accuracy of the Bible (Israeli archaeologists depend heavily on the Bible to guide them to specific areas to research and study). Outside the natural realm, we have the astounding reality of the prophetic reliability of the Bible.

And the genius of establishing and maintaining the authenticity of the original still astounds.

But what about Jonah's three days in the belly of the fish? What about the miracles and the resurrection? Going back to our logical law of inference, we can state that in the areas testable by scientific tests (archaeological and historical) the Bible is accurate and valid. We can also state that the current copies of the Bible are authentic copies of the original. And we can say that biblical prophecies have proven to be true and accurate. We can therefore conclude that those parts of the Bible not tested or testable are also true.

Since the Bible was written in the past, it is history. We know that anything in the realm of history cannot meet the test for absolute truth. In this case, therefore, we must resort to the laws of probability. We know that the stronger the evidence supporting the probability, the closer we approach the certainty of absolute truth. The probability of truth generally relies on one or more of the following: eyewitness testimony, reliable documentation, scientific confirmation, and historical confirmation. We must keep in mind that the more objective the evidence, the more reliable it is.

In the Bible, we have all the above. The authors of the Bible were for the most part eyewitnesses to the events they documented. The authenticity and reliability of the documentation has been repeatedly proven. Archaeological (scientific) proof abounds. The historical value and authenticity have been attested to by the Israelis and others time and again. Many of the tests were conducted by those trying to disprove the reliability and authenticity of the Bible. You cannot get more objective than that!

So with complete confidence, we can say the Bible meets the highest level of rational probability possible so much so that any rational mind would conclude that the secular proof presented approaches absolute truth. Yes, the Bible is a truthful and reliable document.

Part 3 will provide more in-depth information on the topics above.

# Chapter 4

Most of us have experienced major events in our lives that we have pigeonholed in remote corners of our minds because we didn't understand their implications or importance. The following is one such event that had not one but two life-threatening episodes that could have cost the lives of at least four of us, but the Almighty had a better plan.

**August 1980 In Southwest New Mexico at 13,000 feet.**

The back of my shirt was damp from perspiration. Though late August in the southwestern part of the United States is always hot, most of the perspiration was not from the heat.

A few days earlier, three of my air force friends, Oz, Andy, Rick, and I had decided to fly from our home station, Luke Air Force Base near Phoenix, to El Paso for the day. We rented a Cessna 172, a four-seater, and early one cool morning, we took off and were on our way. With the exception of our approach to the El Paso airport, the three-hour flight was very routine, uneventful, and enjoyable. Flying through and just over the mountains early in the morning in the American Southwest is always awe inspiring. The moving shadows and subtle changes in colors in the deep valleys and steep mountain walls accentuated by the rising sun is something that has to be experienced to be appreciated. Just awesome!

About thirty miles from the airport, I called the tower, identified myself, and requested landing instructions. We were approaching El Paso from the west, the airport was ahead and to our left, and the Mexican border was below us just slightly to our right.

We were at 6,500 feet (since the airport was 3,962 feet above sea level, that meant we were about 2,500 above ground level, or AGL). The tower gave us our heading and directed us to maintain altitude. I adjusted our heading accordingly and noticed that an air force C-130 had just taken off (the airport was used by civilian and military aircraft) and was heading our way. I maintained my heading and altitude while keeping an eye on the C-130, but it was not moving! When you're in the air and see another airborne object that doesn't appear to be moving but appears to be getting larger, that means only one thing—you're on collision course!

I called the tower and informed them of my concern. I could detect a certain degree of urgency in the controller's voice when he emphatically stated, "Cessna 347 initiate an immediate right three hundred and sixty and descend to six thousand feet." Before he had finished his instructions, I dipped my right wing and applied right rudder while lowering the nose. As I nosedived into Mexican airspace, I hoped that the C-130 had also been given similar evasive instructions. I leveled off at 2,000 feet AGL and proceeded through 180 degrees of the turn. Looking through the upper-right-hand portion of our windshield, I noticed the receding underbelly of the 130 as it made a climbing right turn. How close did we get? At the time it seemed like 200, 300 feet. More than likely it was probably over 500 feet.

The landing on that long runway was uneventful. It was almost 10:30 in the morning when we tied down the aircraft. As the fuel truck approached, I did a quick mental calculation and figured that we had better not top off the tanks because the temperature was going to be near 100 (a small and relatively underpowered airplane does not climb well in hot air) when we planned to leave around 3:00 that afternoon. And truth be known, not one of us was less than the 170 pounds the load computation manual used for the average passenger weight for our plane. Hoping to shave some 120 pounds off our gross takeoff weight, I instructed the fuel truck driver to just fill it two-thirds full. He agreed, and we took off to explore El Paso and Juarez, Mexico. Oz was from El Paso, so he was our official guide. I had only one note of caution—don't buy anything bulky or heavy.

Close to two o'clock, we began to wrap it up. There had been some discussion that since we had not bought anything heavy, perhaps we could take back a container of tamales from Juarez. We had had some for lunch, and they were good. Rather reluctantly I agreed; we bought the tamales. The container was perhaps fourteen inches wide and maybe two feet tall and weighed perhaps thirty pounds. We headed to the airport.

Knowing we would be close to our maximum weight on takeoff, I was extra careful on my preflight inspection. Everything was going great until I got to the fuel check. Contrary to my instructions, the tanks were full! I contacted the fuel section and asked them to remove a third of the fuel. They apologized and said they would get on it as soon as they could—in about two or three hours! More mental calculations. The wind? From the east, five, six knots. Temperature? 101. Runway? Over ten thousand feet, with an easterly takeoff run. It was close but doable. I decided to go. We boarded, got clearance to the taxiway, and did our run-up check. I got clearance from the tower to enter the runway and proceed with takeoff.

Knowing our situation, I decided to use short-runway takeoff procedures. The time was 3:11 with a nearly cloudless sky. I held the brakes down hard, took the engine to 100 percent, popped the brakes off, and the airplane jumped forward. Normal takeoff speed is about sixty-five knots, but I wanted a minimum of eighty-five to make sure we had enough lift. But it didn't feel we were gaining speed fast enough. At the 5,000-foot marker, we were going through just sixty knots, and the heat coming off the runway had to be way over 110 degrees! At the 7,000-foot marker, we were approaching eighty knots.

I had set the go/no go point at 8,500; otherwise, there wouldn't have been enough runway left to abort. At the 8,000-foot marker, we passed eighty-five knots, I held the nose down, and some 500 feet before the 9,000-foot marker I jerked the nose up and at the same time the stall warning horn blared out! I pushed the nose down to straight and level flight. We were about twenty feet in the air; taking advantage of ground effect (at speed and close to the ground you will almost always get better lift), we cleared the fences and some small outbuildings. Our airspeed was inching up to 100 knots when the stall warning stopped. I jerked the nose up quickly and the stall warning blared out even louder, but we gained another 100 feet before I dropped the nose again. Noting some patchy clouds in front, I started cloud jumping to take advantage of the thermals.

I continued dropping the nose to straight and level flight, gaining speed, jerking the nose up, and cloud jumping until we got to 6,500 feet, about 2,500 AGL. Hot air can really impede a small airplane's climbing ability. On hot, sunny days, a cloud's shadow can generate a significant amount of thermals, which can help you gain altitude. After reaching altitude, I made a right 180, contacted the tower, and advised them of my intentions. We headed for the mountain pass near the Mexican border. This time, we did not invade their airspace. Time? 3:19.

After we crossed the pass, we were at cruising speed but still climbing very slowly, and we had higher mountains ahead. We had to climb to at least 12,000 feet to clear all mountains between us and Phoenix. Then I noticed that the plane was exceedingly quiet other than the sound of the engine; there was not a sound from anybody—nobody had said a word!

I looked at the three passengers; their eyes were fixed on me. I grinned. Then I couldn't stop them from talking! Oz, sitting in the right front seat, broke the silence by saying, "I knew we were in some kind of trouble when that horn blared out right after we took off. I looked out the window and I swear I was staring into somebody's basement!" Andy said something to the effect that when I was raising and lowering the nose and that incessant horn kept blaring out, he wondered if maybe he would have to throw out the tamales to lighten the load. But he said that after some deep thought, he realized he couldn't throw out the tamales, which meant only one thing—Rick would have to go!

We made it back to Phoenix safely; somebody had been watching over us. We had a great time, and we ate the tamales in a matter of days. To this day we refer to this trip as the "Tamale Run."

In those short eight minutes that seemed a lifetime, we all learned something about ourselves. I'm not sure all the passengers were aware of how dicey the situation had been, but I believe Oz was. Sometime after the trip, I asked him why he had been so quiet at the beginning of our return trip. He said he looked at me and noticed how intent and absorbed I was about halfway down the runway. When he noticed the beads of sweat on my forehead and eyebrows, he knew there was no way he was going to interrupt my concentration.

I had fallen prey to the very temptation I repeatedly cautioned my students about— don't push the envelope unless it's an emergency situation! This was but one of many situations we have been involved in that I believe has immeasurably contributed to our continuing friendship.

Many years later, back in San Antonio, one of our conversations got around to Jesus and the Bible. After much discussion, Oz stated that he believed Jesus was a good man and a good, moral teacher but that he didn't think he ever claimed to be God. At that time, I was not conversant enough with the Bible to counter his assessment. The following is a brief answer to that statement. A part of God's plan?

# Wasn't Jesus Just a Good Man and a Good, Moral Teacher?

Generally, this question normally includes something to the effect that he probably was a prophet but not God and never claimed to be God. Let's take a look at these components:

*Jesus was a good man.* A caveat here: although secular history gives us a significant amount of information on the man Jesus, this discussion will to a large part depend on the information in scripture. If you doubt the validity and authenticity of the Bible, read part 4. We won't spend any time discussing whether Jesus existed. The secular record, which includes the writings of Tacitus, Flavius Josephus, the Talmud, Julius Africanus, Lucian, Eliezar, Mara Bar-Serapion, and Pliny the Younger and others provide ample secular evidence of his existence.

In describing Jesus, Matthew wrote that he had a compassionate nature (he fed the hungry, healed the sick, and so on). Mark wrote that he was kind, selfless, focused, serious, and pleased to serve people. Paul described him as obedient to his Father's wishes. Luke wrote that Jesus had a merciful, forgiving, and loving heart. John described him as honest and truthful and he said that he lived a life we could follow explicitly. Peter said he was patient, "patient toward you, not wishing for any to perish, but for all to come to repentance" (2 Peter 3:9).

Jesus definitely drew people to him. It was not his strong, chiseled face or muscular, handsome physique or great oratory skills, for as attested to by the prophet Isaiah (53:2), he had "no beauty or majesty to attract us to him, nothing in his appearance that we should desire him." No, it was his personality, character, and message that drew the crowds to him. Jesus was a good man.

***Jesus was a good, moral teacher.*** If when we make this statement, we believe that among his other qualities and claims he was also a good, moral teacher, we are on solid ground. However, if we believe that at best he was a good, moral teacher, we have a problem.

To address the belief that at best Jesus was just a good, moral teacher and not God, I turn to C. S. Lewis's *Mere Christianity.*

> I am trying here to prevent anyone from saying the really foolish thing that people often say about Him: 'I'm ready to accept Jesus as a great moral teacher, but I don't accept his claim to be God.' That is the one thing we must not say. A man who was merely a man and said the sort of things Jesus said would not be a great moral teacher. He would either be a lunatic—on a level with a man who says he is a poached egg—or else He would be the Devil of hell. You must make your choice. Either this man was, and is, the Son of God, or else a madman or something worse. You can either shut Him up for a fool, you can spit at Him and kill Him as a demon; or you can fall at his feet and call Him Lord and God. But let us not come up with any patronizing nonsense about his being a great human teacher. He has not left that option open to us. He did not intend to.

***Did Jesus claim to be God?*** In John 10, we find Jesus walking in Solomon's Colonnade, a part of the temple courts. As was usual, Jews gathered around him, and they asked him if he was the Messiah. Jesus answered, "I and the Father are one." When they picked up stones to stone him, he asked them for which of his good deeds were they prepared to stone him. They responded that they were not stoning him for any of his good deeds but because he, a mere man, was claiming to be God. Scripture says that Jesus eluded their grasp.

In another example, in John 8, Jesus was talking with the temple Jews about Abraham and death. In verse 51, Jesus said, "Very truly I tell you, whoever obeys my word will never see death." The Jews countered, saying that Abraham and all the prophets had died [of course the Jews were talking about physical death but Jesus was talking about spiritual death]. When Jesus said that Abraham rejoiced at the thought of seeing my [the birth, ministry, death and resurrection of Jesus] day; he saw it and was glad. The Jews, visibly upset, shouted that Jesus was not yet fifty, so how could he claim to have seen Abraham! In verse 58, Jesus answered, "Very truly I tell you, before Abraham was born, I AM!" Again the Jews tried to stone him, but Jesus slipped away. We should note that Jesus didn't say "I was" or "I will be"; he said, "I AM." The Bible first records that name when, at the burning bush, God said to Moses, "I AM WHO I AM." The Jews clearly understood that Jesus was claiming to be the eternal God.

Yes, Jesus was a good man, and yes, he was a good, moral teacher, but above all, he was and is the eternal God.

Additional, in-depth information is available in part 3.

# Chapter 5

I had recently completed the year-long RCIA (Roman Catholic Indoctrination for Adults) course. It was very informative, inspiring, and uplifting. I had been raised in an evangelical Christian home. However, after going to college and joining the military, I had drifted away from Christianity. Many years later, my wife wanted me to join the Catholic Church. Since we had not been attending any church, I responded to the prompting of a close friend and mentor who offered to sponsor me and agreed to attend the course.

After completing the course, I was confident of and pleased with the knowledge I had received. So what was that nagging feeling in the back of my mind? I had a working knowledge of the sacraments, church doctrine, church hierarchy, and some history of the popes, so why the uneasiness? It came to me that I knew more about the Catholic Church than the church I had been brought up in. I decided to remedy that.

That started the continuing research into the church from biblical times to the present. The study was relatively straightforward until I got to the Reformation. After that, the research began to get unwieldy. Worldwide, there are hundreds of denominations under the Protestant umbrella. The only real common denominator in the "Christian" community, including the Catholic Church, is the Bible. But even within that common denominator, there is a significant difference in how the Bible is interpreted.

Having come to the understanding that even though there are some differences between denominations, there is no doubt that the Bible is the common binder. As I was going through this research, questions kept coming up in my mind that revolved around Christianity itself. Who is a Christian? What is a Christian? As you observe the various "Christians" and their beliefs, who's right? They all claim the Bible as their authority. I then turned the efforts of my research into trying to answer the question, what is a Christian?

Of course my research started with the Bible. I also accessed many Christian books through the Logos Christian Library. The Christian Apologetics Research Ministry and the Christian Research Institute were also very valuable resources. I studied the doctrinal statements of the major denominations; I compared doctrinal beliefs to various lists of essential Christian principles codified by historical biblical scholars. I was pleasantly surprised to find a great similarity between almost all the lists. Those principles that had clear biblical references, that were clearly stated by the authors as essential beliefs, and that had a clear emphasis throughout the Bible are listed below.

# What Is a Christian?

The Bible is very explicit and definitive in the guidance it provides. Each of the following principles is presented in the Bible without any doubt or equivocation as to its criticality. We do need to understand that this is not a roadmap to salvation (obtaining eternal life) but a list of essential truths believers accept. The Christian Apologetic Research Ministry refers to their lists as Primary Essentials of Christianity, followed by their Secondary Essentials of Christianity, and so on.[1] These principles are primarily intended to help you and

---

[1] You can explore them at CARM.org.

provide assurance that you are progressing in your Christian life in accordance with the guidance provided by the Bible

A Christian is a person who believes in Jesus Christ (more discussion on how to become a Christian is presented in the part on "Christianity"). The Bible provides those who believe in Jesus abundant guidance and assistance. A Christian accepts and believes the following truths, all of which are equally important.

## Monotheism

Throughout humanity's history, there has been a tendency to turn to a visible god, most often a god made of gold or silver. In all cases, this god was made by human hands. Other times, people turned to animals or inanimate objects such as mountains, trees, or even celestial bodies. The Bible states that people will call other people or objects gods, but there is only one true God, the God of Abraham, Isaac, and Jacob, the biblical God, the Creator of the universe and all there is or ever will be.

How important is this principle? Well, God wrote it as his first commandment: "You shall have no other Gods before me" (Exodus 20:3). God said, "Before me no God was formed, nor will there be one after me" (Isaiah 43:10). God also stated, "I am the first and I am the last; apart from me there is no God" (Isaiah 44:6). There are many such references throughout the Bible.

## The Trinity

Although readily defined, One God represented in three distinct persons—God the Father, God the Son, and God the Holy Spirit. Getting your mind around this concept is difficult at best if indeed possible at all. Although there is no specific verse in the Bible that is translatable to the definition given, the Bible is replete with references to the Trinity; the first is in Genesis 1:26; before Adam and Eve were created, God said, "Let *us* make mankind in *our* image, in *our* likeness" [my emphasis]. In the New Testament (Matthew 28:19), Jesus said, "baptizing them in the name of the Father and of the Son and of the Holy Spirit." There are many more references to the concept of the Trinity throughout the scriptures.

## Jesus' Divinity

In most arguments of reason, there is often what is called the "discriminator," a fact that will usually determine the outcome of the argument. Jesus' divinity is a critical principle that definitely fits this definition. You cannot claim to be a Christian and deny Jesus' divinity, the knowledge that God came to dwell among humanity in the flesh in the form of Jesus. The incarnate Jesus was fully God and fully human. The apostle John, when cautioning believers about whose teachings to believe, put it this way in his first epistle (1 John 4:1–3).

> Dear friends, do not believe every spirit, but test the spirits to see whether they are from God, because many false prophets have gone out into the world. This is how you can recognize the Spirit of God: Every spirit that acknowledges that Jesus Christ has come in the flesh is from God, but every spirit that does not acknowledge Jesus is not from God.

All non-Christians deny that Jesus is God, a definite discriminator.

## The Gospel

Almost all the New Testament is devoted to the gospel of Jesus Christ. The apostle John started our understanding of the gospel with his writing in John 1:1, 3, 10–12.

> In the beginning was the Word [Jesus] and the Word
> was with God, and the Word was God. Through him
> all things were made, without him nothing was made
> that has been made. He was in the world, and though
> the world was made through him, the world did not
> recognize him. He came to that which was his own, but
> his own did not receive him. Yet to all who did receive
> him, to those who believed in his name, he gave the right
> to become children of God.

The apostle Paul, in what has been accepted as one of the first New Testament books written (scholars believe it was penned around AD 45–50, less than twenty years after the crucifixion of Jesus), defined the gospel rather concisely in 1 Corinthians 15:1–8.

> Now, brothers and sisters, I want to remind you of the
> gospel … I passed on to you as of first importance: that
> Christ died for our sins according to the Scriptures,
> that he was buried, that he was raised on the third day
> according to the Scriptures, and that he appeared to
> Cephas, and then to the Twelve. After that he appeared
> to more than five hundred of the brothers and sisters at
> the same time, most of whom are still living, though
> some have fallen asleep. Then he appeared to James,
> then to all the apostles, and last of all he appeared to
> me also.

The James referred to by Paul is Jesus' brother who, according to the scriptures, not only did not believe what Jesus had been preaching but also considered Jesus mentally unstable (John 7:5): "For even his own brothers did not believe in him." Prior to becoming an apostle, Peter had been known as Cephas. This gospel reference also became one of the first doctrines of the new church.

In a later writing, Paul reiterated the importance of the gospel quite emphatically in Galatians 1:7–9.

Evidently some people ... are trying to pervert the Gospel of Christ. But even if we or an angel from heaven should preach a gospel other than the one we preached to you, let them be under God's curse! As we have already said, so now I say again: If anybody is preaching to you a gospel other than what you accepted, let them be under God's curse!

In summary, the gospel is that Jesus is God in the flesh who died for our sins, rose from the dead, and through his grace freely gives the gift of eternal life to those who believe in him.

## The Bodily Resurrection of Christ

Shortly after Jesus' crucifixion, some believed his resurrection was only in the spirit. Among those who believed this were the Gnostics, who believed that everything spiritual was good while everything material (such as our bodies) was intrinsically evil. Early Christians found this troubling since they already believed the soul was eternal. Thus a resurrection in only the spirit would be no resurrection at all. No, the resurrection of Christ was in the body. Jesus appeared to the apostles right after his resurrection.

They were startled and frightened, thinking they saw a ghost. He said to them, "Why are you troubled, and why do doubts rise in your minds? Look at my hands and my feet. It is I myself! Touch me and see, a ghost does not have flesh and bones, as you see I have." (Luke 24:37–39)

Later that evening, Jesus ate with them; he did so as further proof of his physical presence. Paul also addressed these concerns to the Corinthians by flatly stating that if Christ had not been raised from the dead, Paul's preaching was useless, their faith was useless, and therefore they would all still be in their sins. But no, Jesus had indeed been raised from the dead. He had appeared to his apostles who touched him and ate with him. He then appeared to hundreds, and he had also appeared to Paul himself. Jesus was but the first fruits of those who would be raised from the dead, his believers.

## Salvation by Grace

Those religions that believe in the afterlife all believe that whether you enter into the "good" afterlife or not is dependent on what you do in this life. If you continually do good things, you might get into the good afterlife; if you do bad things in this life, you will go to the "other" place. Only Christianity believes whether you enter into the good afterlife depends on what you believe. This belief comes from our understanding that all humanity is so steeped in sin that people are incapable of doing anything that would come close to preparing them to meet the righteousness required by God for entry into his presence. Knowing this, God, not wanting anyone to perish, sent his Son to pay the ultimate sacrifice for our sins. Jesus was the only one able to pay for our sins as he was sinless and without blemish. All that would be required of us was to believe in him through faith and that he died in our place and to accept his grace. Once we believe, we will want to do good works because we will have a desire to be more like him.

Scripture is replete with references to salvation by faith through grace; many biblical authors wrote about it, but the apostle Paul was the most prolific writer on the subject. Keeping in mind that whenever a writer refers to "works" or the "law," he is referring to what you do, we will start with the apostle Paul (Romans 3:22, 28): "Righteousness is given through faith in Jesus to all who believe." He continued, "For we maintain that a person is justified [meets the requirements for salvation] by faith apart from the works of the law." In Galatians 2:16, 21 he wrote, "We … have put our faith in Christ

Jesus that we may be justified by faith in Christ and not by the works of the law, because by the works of the law no one will be justified." He emphasized that "if righteousness could be gained through the law, Christ died for nothing." In Ephesians 2:8–9, he stated, "For it is by grace you have been saved, through faith—and this is not from yourselves, it is the gift of God—not by works, so that no one can boast." The apostle John concluded his first epistle with, "I write these things to you who believe in the name of the Son of God so that you may know that you have eternal life" (1 John 5:13).

One of the most chilling statements in the Bible comes from Jesus as he concluded the Sermon on the Mount. In referring to the day of judgment, he said, "Many will say to me on that day, 'Lord, Lord, did we not prophesy in your name and in your name drive out demons and in your name perform many miracles?' Then I will tell them plainly, 'I never knew you. Away from me, you evildoers!'" (Matthew 7:22–23). What gives? Will they not have done all these great things for Jesus, yet he will deny them? This reference certainly underlines that it is not what you do, it is what you believe. These people were really wrapped up in what they did (I did this, I did that), and not once did they say they believed nor did they ask for forgiveness. The Bible does not equivocate—salvation is by grace alone.

## Jesus—The Way to God

The concept that the only way to God is through Jesus has been called [primarily by those that believe that truth is relative] the "scandalous exclusivity of Christianity." Scandalous or not, the Bible leaves no room for doubt. Right after the Last Supper in the upper room in Jerusalem, the night before his crucifixion, Jesus comforted his disciples. He had told them he was going away, but

I will come back and take you with me that you also may be where I am. You know the way to the place where I am going. Thomas said to him, "Lord, we don't know where you are going, so how can we know the way?" Jesus answered, "I am the way and the truth and the life. No one comes to the Father except through me." (John 14:6)

This passage needs no interpretation.

# Chapter 6

**Houston, Texas, October 2012**

The evening was crisp and cool as we sat out in my friend's backyard. The day had been good. The golf in the morning was enjoyable; no problems with the drives (for us, drives in the 180 to 220 range were good; we set our own standards) or the putting; just some minor flubs in the chipping department (chipping had never been my strong suit). After a good meal at one of Houston's many Vietnamese restaurants, we were musing about the day and the camaraderie we shared. As we were prone to do, we shifted our conversation to Christianity.

That time, the discussion centered around Mormons, Protestants, and Roman Catholics. We talked about how all three had God as their deity and how each claimed a relationship with Jesus. This being the case, what were the differences? The following is the crux of our discussion with added references. Understanding that the Protestant umbrella is quite expansive as are their nonessential beliefs, we will discuss the Protestants from the perspective of the Christians who adhere to the core doctrines written about in the preceding question.

# Do Mormons, Catholics, and Protestants Have the Same Beliefs?

For some perspective on this question, we'll take a look at some 2010 statistics. Of the approximate 2.1 billion proclaimed adherents to Christianity worldwide, some 1.2 billion are Catholic, with the remainder falling into the Protestant category. Within this category, the major groups are the Pentecostals (279 million), Baptists (110 million), nondenominational (80 million), Lutherans (75 million), Methodists (75 million), and Reformed (75 million). The Mormons, a much newer religion founded in the 1800s by Joseph Smith, has a much smaller following of approximately 13 million. It is, however very aggressive in spreading its teachings and is experiencing significant growth.

We will start our discussion by summarizing the key beliefs of each of the three groups. We should understand that the reason most people become members of a church and worship is to understand how to assure themselves of a good afterlife and to do what it takes to receive that assurance. I believe, therefore, that an explanation of how each church group addresses the concept of salvation is key in our discussion.

**Mormons**

In the early 1800s, Joseph Smith, while praying, was given revelations from God, leading to the Book of Mormon. The angel told Joseph that the churches he had been attending were abominations and that his revelations were to replace the corrupted Bible. When Joseph Smith first started spreading Mormonism in the early 1820s, his sermons seemed to accept the concept of a single god. By the 1840s, his sermons began to espouse a concept of progression from man to god.

Brigham Young, the second Mormon prophet, Joseph Smith's successor, stated in his writings, "Man is king of kings and lord of lords in embryo." And in the Journal of Discourse 3:93, he wrote, "The Lord created you and me for the purpose of becoming gods like himself. We are created to become gods like unto our father in heaven."

Joseph Fielding Smith, the tenth Mormon prophet, explained this concept: "Our father in heaven, according to the prophet, had a father, and since there has been a condition of this kind through all eternity, each father had a father."

With the acceptance of this concept, the Plan of Eternal Progression, Mormons must believe there is an infinite number of gods and gods in the making. Mormons summarize this belief with the following: "As man is, god once was. As god is, man may become."

The progression, god the father (a man of flesh and bones just like us) used to be a man on another planet; he became a god by following the dictates of the god of his planet. Being a god, he was given this world as his own. With his goddess wife, he produced offspring in heaven. Jesus was his firstborn, then the devil, and then all of us. We were spirit offspring who eventually inhabited newborns on earth; we then forgot all about our first birth.

If we become faithful Mormons, tithe the full 10 percent of our income, and adhere to all the rules of the Mormon Church, we too have the potential of becoming gods of our own planets and starting the process all over again.

The Mormon Church believes that you are saved by grace, after all you can do. The all you can do includes denying yourself all ungodliness, turning from all sins and committing them no more, living the Ten Commandments, loving all others, praying for our adversaries, clothing the naked, feeding the hungry, living chaste and clean lives, and being completely honest in all your dealings. Once you are saved by grace, you must continue to live without sin or you will lose your salvation. When you combine these requirements, the church is actually requiring that you must be without sin to be able to receive grace. All very commendable, but is it humanly possible?

## Catholics

In general matters of the Bible (notwithstanding the inclusion of most of the Apocrypha in the Catholic Old Testament at the Council of Trent in the mid-1500s), Catholics and Protestants share a great degree of similarity. One of the major differences comes in the additional source of authority for the church. Church authority is derived equally from the traditions of the church as well as the Bible. Church members are encouraged to read the Bible and are free to interpret it as their consciences dictate if it does not conflict with the interpretation of the church. The magisterium is the final interpretive biblical authority for the church.

Another major difference between most Protestant churches and the Catholic Church is in its adoption of many nonbiblical beliefs and practices. Examples include purgatory, the veneration of Mary, the Immaculate Conception, intercessory prayers to Mary and the saints, the Eucharist, the seven sacraments, absolution, and iconic statutes in places of worship. Many of these nonbiblical practices can be traced to the early church after Emperor 'Constantine declared Christianity the state religion.

The worship of the god Mithras was the religion of many Romans, including most soldiers, before Christianity. To receive salvation, they would eat a sacrificial meal of raw flesh and drink the blood of a young bull in which their God was "present." Mithraism also had seven sacraments.

Another large segment of the Roman population, including most of the emperors, were henotheists; they believed in one supreme god over many lesser gods. These lesser gods would be "in charge" of certain other things by which they would be known, such as the god of love, god of peace, god of war, god of strength, and so on.

Origen, an early church father, lived in Alexandria, Egypt, the center of the cult of Isis, a mother goddess also known as the Queen of Heaven and the Mother of God. Catholic Mariology can be traced back to the writings of Origen.

From a lay perspective, the links between Mariology and Isis, the Eucharist with the "presence" of Jesus in the host, the seven sacraments and Mithraism, and the Catholic saints with the "lesser gods" of the henotheists are quite compelling. It can be realistically concluded that the inclusion of these nonbiblical practices in Christian worship was to make it more appealing for these "other" practitioners to be assimilated into the new state church. If it was, it worked; the church experienced rapid growth during this period.

Catholics are saved by receiving grace from God that enables them to believe in Christ and the truth of the Catholic Church. When they are baptized, they are infused by grace, which leads to their justification and salvation. To maintain salvation and the infused (sanctifying) grace, they must participate in the sacraments. This infused grace can be lessened (but not lost) by the commission of venial sins or completely lost by the commission of mortal sins.

After the commission of venial sins, the infused grace can be restored by partaking of the Eucharist [Holy Communion] and the performance of penance [some act normally prescribed by a priest] in perfect contrition and absolved by a priest in confession. Though absolved, the punishment due because of the sin remains and can be removed only by indulgence(s). The church teaches that it is possible to regain salvation after the commission of mortal sins but only after a considerably longer and more intensive penitent process.

**Protestants**

Bible-based Christian churches adhere to the teachings of scripture that state that salvation is achieved by what we believe, not what we do. We are incapable of doing anything, no matter how good, merciful, benevolent, generous, or loving the acts may be, that would make us worthy of entrance into heaven.

Because God is holy, he cannot tolerate sin, and we are inherently sinful. On our own, we would never be able to gain entry into God's presence. Knowing this, God, not wanting anyone to perish, sent his Son to pay the ultimate sacrifice for our sins. Jesus was the only one able to pay for our sins as he was sinless and without blemish. All that would be required of us would be to believe in him through faith that he died in our place and to accept his grace. Once we believe, he cloaks us with his own righteousness, thus enabling us to be worthy of heaven. After salvation, we will want to do good works because we will have a desire to be more like him.

To summarize, here are the essential principles of Christianity.

- One God
- the Trinity (Father, Son, and Holy Spirit)
- the deity of Christ
- the gospel
- resurrection in the body
- salvation by grace alone
- accepting that the only way to the Father is through the Son.

Mormonism essentially rejects all these beliefs. Catholicism requires works before justification and salvation. So no, the three churches do not have the same core beliefs. Some vary a lot, some not so much.

# Part 2:

## The Basics

# Overview of Part 2

In this part, we will go over a few rules, standards, and laws necessary to establish the validity of the belief systems we will review.

## Worldviews

These consist of the presuppositions that are supported by truth claims. Worldviews determine how we as individuals interpret all received data.

## Presuppositions

Because we are not all knowing, when we are given information to understand, we have to resort to assumptions. These assumptions are presuppositions.

## Truth and Truth Claims

What is truth? How do we define it? While some believe truth can and does mean different things to different people or cultures, these differing interpretations are actually truth claims. Truth claims are what people perceive as being true. To define truth, we will need to look at three concepts

***The Correspondence Theory of Truth.*** This basic theory is fundamental to our understanding of truth.

***First Principles.*** The concept of first principles is key to arriving at truth in much of our daily life.

***Logic.*** Logic will help us put things in perspective and make it easier for us to arrive at truth, i.e., to make sense of things.

We will then move from defining truth to the application of truth in our everyday lives and how we use it in practically everything we do.

***Absolute Truth.*** What we all want.

***Possibility of Truth.*** We will take a quick look at this rather tenuous principle.

***Probability of Truth.*** This is a very important principle and requires a more in-depth review.

This review concludes with a short discussion on a basic law of physics.

## Basic Physics

Energy, work, and the decay of functionality is best expressed in what we know as the laws of thermodynamics.

# Chapter 7

# How We See and Understand the World

## Worldviews

A young man in a middle-class suburban neighborhood is walking home from his late-evening job and sees a policeman approaching him on a dimly lit sidewalk. Terrified, he wants to run, but there is no place to go. He takes a deep breath. Every fiber of his body is coiled. He is ready to flee, but he continues to walk toward the policeman. His eyes fixate on the menacing .45 on the officer's hip.

The officer looks at him, smiles, and says, "Have a good evening, son," and walks past him. The young man nods, relaxes, and exhales as reality begins to flood his being. He is no longer in his home country, Sierra Leone. Relieved, his eyes begin to well up as visions of continual atrocities race through his memory, atrocities his family, relatives, friends, and fellow villagers suffered at the hands of policemen.

We all take the data we receive and consciously or subconsciously processes it through a subjective standard we call a worldview. This standard acts as a filter that screens, analyzes, and categorizes all this information. Without this filter, information received would be completely meaningless because there would be no frame of reference for it to help us decide what's true and what's false for us; it helps us make rational decisions (at least rational to us), and it is our guide for establishing the values and ethics we live by.

The young man in the example above had a well-defined worldview of armed policemen. He didn't analyze, reason, or have any foreknowledge of his presuppositions or his truth claims. He just knew the best course of action when he saw an armed policeman was to flee!

## Presuppositions

Worldviews are based on presuppositions, which may also be called assumptions. As members of the human race (regardless of the cultures or environments we come from), some of our presuppositions are similar. Some of these include the desire to protect and care for our young, the supposition that killing another person is normally not appropriate, and so on.

On the other hand, some very diverse worldviews exist in this world. Normally, the most diverse worldviews tend to come from different people whose cultures have had minimal or no contact with each other. That is not to say people who live close to others will normally have the same or even similar worldviews; on the contrary, people in the United States have very diverse backgrounds, cultures, and worldviews, and most believe that contributes to our strength, stability, and durability.

So in addition to the factors above, our presuppositions are influenced by our ethnicity, parents, siblings, neighborhoods, education, religious experience, and other life factors.

In the worldview of the young man from Sierra Leone, armed policemen were not to be trusted; this was a presupposition based on his experience. Were his truth claims valid?

## Truth Claims

Each presupposition is supported by one or more truth claims, but these are not necessarily true. The truth claims that support our presuppositions that in turn support our worldview(s) are taken for granted; we do not analyze, discuss, or defend them because we accept them, and to us they are true.

A person's worldview determines what is reality to that person. A worldview supported by presuppositions based on erroneous truth claims will not lead people to actual truth but to what they perceive as truth. That is why two people who have different worldviews when given the same data will often reach different conclusions.

In the young man's world of Sierra Leone, the truth claim that policemen hurt, kill, and maim innocent people was indeed valid and supported his worldview in that country. However, that worldview was not supported by universally valid truth claims. The policeman is an instrument of government whose role is to enforce the laws and rules of society and to protect the innocent and helpless in that society. Is this role sometimes misused? Unfortunately, it sometimes is. However, this does not change the intended universal role.

If we have two people who wear glasses and one person's prescription is correct (true), what that person visualizes will represent reality. If the other person's prescription is not correct, what that person visualizes will not represent reality. Therefore, if we can show that the presuppositions supporting a person's worldview are based on false truth claims, thereby creating a high probability that the presupposition is also false, we should be able to show that person that any belief or reality dependent upon that worldview is also false.

So how do we determine if the presuppositions supporting any particular worldview may be based on false truth claims? There are several tests we can consider.

- Consistency. Are the presuppositions consistent with each other?
- Lifestyle errors. Does the supported worldview endorse a lifestyle that is in our best interest?
- Satisfying. Does the supported worldview provide emotional and spiritual satisfaction?
- Needs. Does the supported worldview satisfy our instinctive human needs?
- Answers. Does the supported worldview answer the crucial questions, Where did I come from? Why am I here? Where will I go when I die?

If the worldview in question meets the tests mentioned, it has a very high probability of being based on reality, hence truthful. If it doesn't meet these tests, the truth claims supporting the suppositions are suspect.

## Summary

Everything we think, see, or perceive is filtered through our worldview based on presuppositions formed by our experiences and environment. These presuppositions are affirmed by truth claims.

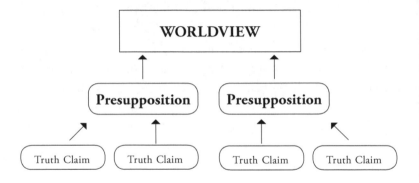

In the following chapter, we will look at additional tests based on scientific methods and on adherence to some basic laws of physics.

# Chapter 8

# Defining Truth

## The Correspondence Theory of Truth

Truth is real; it cannot change. Truth not only corresponds to reality, it is reality. We can look to Aristotle (384–322 BC), undoubtedly one of the best-known Greek philosophers, who explained this concept best in his Metaphysics: "To say that that which is, is not or that which is not is, is a falsehood; and to say that that which is, is and that which is not, is not, is truth." Truth is what is real, the way things are regardless of what we think or what we want them to be.

I often read in my study. One quiet evening, while reading, I began to crave a cup of tea. I put my book down, went to the kitchen, and put the kettle on. As I waited for the water to boil, I wondered where I had put my book. On my desk? On the coffee table? For no apparent reason, this became important to me, so I mentally retraced my actions to the time I was reading.

I saw myself dog-ear a page, close the book, and lay it down on the … desk? Yes, yes, of course, the desk. I always lay it down on the desk. That being settled, I went back to making my tea and carried it to my study. I went to my desk, sure the book was there. It was not. It was on the coffee table. Reality did not correspond to my perceived truth.

We know the relationship of truth to reality as the correspondence theory of truth. If we do not accept that truth must correspond to reality, truth cannot exist; it would differ from person to person and from culture to culture. Ultimate reality would be unreachable for us. Even our dependence on science would be suspect because its truth depends on reality.

## First Principles Theory of Truth

Foundational to all thought, knowledge, and reason is the concept known as first principles. One of the first proponents of this principle was René Descartes, a fifteenth-century French philosopher/mathematician considered by many to be the father of modern philosophy.

From among his many interests and studies, we will focus on what is known as his unprejudiced search for the truth. Descartes felt reason to doubt much of the established philosophy; he believed that if he discarded any belief with which he had even the slightest doubt, he would eventually arrive at the truth. Following this long process, he came to the conclusion that the fact that "I exist" is impossible to doubt and is, therefore, absolutely true. So that which exists on its own, requiring no additional support, is true.

His "Cogito, ergo sum" ("I think, therefore I am") is an expression of the indubitability of first-person experience. This process by which Descartes discarded everything he doubted until he reached the truth is now known as Descartes's Cartesian Doubt.

Other examples of first principles include

- What I see exists.
- What I hear are real sounds.
- The past is real.
- A material world outside my mind exists.
- The laws of nature are real and will endure.

Included in the concept of first principles are the laws of logic. We will take a more in-depth look at these laws as we proceed.

These first principles do not stand independent of the correspondence theory of truth in that they underscore that truth does correspond to reality. These principles are universal, self-existing, and self-justifying; they are central to all thought and knowledge. No truth can violate them since all truth depends on these principles. If a truth claim violates these first principles, by definition and simple logic, it is false.

## Discovering Truth through Logic

The laws of logic we will review include

- the law of noncontradiction
- the law of identity
- the law of the excluded middle
- the law of rational inference

These four laws of logic are deemed irrefutable in that in attempting to contradict them, you have to affirm their truth. An example would be a religion that requires us to see beyond logic to find the real truth. However, the thought process that would be required to see beyond logic would have to be logical, thus affirming the certainty and absoluteness of logic.

Another example of the irrefutability of these laws includes the belief of certain religions, sects, or cults that basically claim that morals and ethics are relative and therefore there can be no absolute moral standards or truths. A most revealing question to such a statement would be, "Are you absolutely sure about that?" By definition, they make an absolute statement that refutes their whole concept of relativism!

This general concept of the application of logic had its beginnings in ancient Greece, when Aristotle, Socrates, Plato, and their contemporaries developed means of argument and persuasion still being used today.

C. S. Lewis, a well-known writer and professor at Oxford and Cambridge Universities in the early 1900s, was a proponent of Socrates's method of argument and persuasion. He employed these methods in his teaching, public speaking, and writings. His Socretal Societies are still well known at these universities.

In addition to these laws of logic, we will look briefly at certain statements of truth also called self-evident propositions and self-defining tautologies.

## *The Law of Noncontradiction*

The law of noncontradiction states that something cannot be two different things at the same time and in the same sense. My dog, Suzy, a boxer, cannot be a dog and a cat at the same time; she is either a dog or a cat. If contradictions existed at the same time and in the same sense, black could be white, up would be no different from down, and there would be no difference between truth and falsehoods, on and on. Discussions of truth would be impossible, and facts would forever elude us.

## *The Law of Identity*

The law of identity is a little more straightforward. My dog is a dog. ("A" is "A"). Put another way, an object is identical to itself. Every entity (thing) has an identity; if it has no identity, it is nothing and does not exist.

## *The Law of the Excluded Middle*

The law of the excluded middle is almost as straightforward. Simply put, a statement is either true or false—there is no middle. Some claim that there is a third option, that the truth or falsity of a statement can be unknown. However, being unknown does not negate that it is either true or false; we just have not determined which. But we can rest assured that it will be one or the other, true or false, no middle ground, hence the excluded middle.

These three laws are considered the basic laws in classical logic. However, this does not minimize the importance of the law of rational inference.

## The Law of Rational Inference

The law of rational inference is surely one of the most highly used laws in academia. This law simply states that if I can verify the truthfulness of my premise, I can derive logical and true conclusions from it. I do not have to verify the truthfulness of the conclusion, just the premise(s). For example, "Pigs cannot fly. Mortimer is a pig. Therefore, Mortimer cannot fly." If I accept the truthfulness of the two premises—pigs cannot fly and Mortimer is a pig—I must accept the truthfulness of the conclusion, Mortimer cannot fly. This brings us to the final segment of our discussion on logic.

## Self-Evident Propositions

Self-evident propositions, also known as statements of truth, include,

- If A is shorter than B, B is taller than A.
- Opposites cannot both be true.
- Everything cannot be false.
- Nothing cannot produce something.

## *Self-Defining Tautologies*

A definition of self-defining tautologies is not necessary because they define themselves. Examples of this type of logic would include: all husbands are married, all widows are women, all triangles have three sides.

## Summary

Although animals have a rudimentary ability to think, only humans have the ability to think and reason logically. We do (contrary to the belief of some) live in a rational world, one that subscribes to the laws of logic and other first principles. If we begin to subscribe to belief systems contrary to or that fly in the face of these laws or self-evident truths, doubts will emerge, or at least they should!

At this point, I must stress that if you do not agree that truth (*not* truth claims) corresponds to reality and that the truth you are trying to validate can never violate universal, absolute principles of logic, we might just as well part company.

Truth will forever elude you unless you open your mind and become receptive to these truths that have been a part of humanity since the beginning and the principles of logic known to humanity and clearly defined for us by philosophers several thousand years ago. You will lack the discernment skills necessary to determine truth from falsehood.

In the end, logic, experience, and science don't operate in contradiction, and neither can religion.

# Chapter 9

## Everyday Truth

What is truth? Most Christians recall Pontius Pilate asking that of Christ just before his crucifixion. To this day, most of us have a hard time trying to ascertain truth. If we were to demand absolute truth before we made any everyday decision, or for that matter any decision, our lives would be severely restricted. So how do we decide what is true and what is not true? We have but three options in "accepting truth."

- We can demand absolute truth.
- We can accept the possibility of truth.
- We can make our decisions on the probability of truth.

We should seek the option that provides the highest level of certainty applicable to the area of knowledge in which we are involved. We will shine some light on that shortly, but first let's narrow our options down a little.

The possibility of truth option is rarely if ever a viable choice. If we are unwilling to cross the road until we're sure there is no possibility of being run over, we will never cross the road! We will never eat that hamburger or even that delicious shrimp omelet because of the possibility of being poisoned! So let's get the possibility of truth off the table and work with absolute truth and the probability of truth. If the particular area of knowledge we are working in is mathematical, verifiable through formal logic, or is perceivable in the first person, the highest level of certainty applicable is absolute truth.

Conversely, if the particular areas of knowledge we are working in include one or more of these categories—historical, legal, scientific, philosophical, aesthetic, or religious— the highest level of certainty applicable would be obtained through probability. Of course, the higher the probability, the closer we approach absolute truth. The level of probability is provided by evidence, confirmation of dependability, personal experience, and other information that will help remove reasonable doubt. Know that most of the decisions we make daily are based on the probability that the information they are based on is true.

## Absolute Truth

Each one of us has had experience with people who, when given some information they did not agree with, emphatically stated that unless they had absolute proof it was true, they would not and could not believe it!

If held to that standard, their knowledge universe would indeed be limited. All they could know for certain would be the world of mathematics (seven times seven will always equal forty-nine), some formal logic (triangles will always have three sides), and some limited immediate proximity knowledge they can see, taste, smell, hear, or touch (but our senses can be misled)! So if we venture outside the areas just mentioned, how can we be certain that something is real?

## The Probability of Truth

Determining the probability of truth is the method used by all of us to make almost all decisions requiring knowledge of truth. This is true because almost all our day-to-day decisions are made in the realm of one of these categories: historical (it happened last week but we can't go back to verify), legal (eyewitnesses have conflicting stories), scientific, philosophical, aesthetic, or religious.

The truth we accept through this method is only as dependable as the soundness of the evidence supporting it. What is good evidence? It is evidence that provides sufficient proof to satisfy an unprejudiced mind beyond any reasonable doubt. Make a note of the words *unprejudiced* and *reasonable*. Satisfactory evidence would include eyewitness testimony, reliable documentation, and scientific and historical confirmation. The most reliable probability is that which is based on objective evidence.

In any case, proof for any worldview in the areas of knowledge specified cannot rise above rational probability. The mainstay of this scientific method is inductive reasoning, which by definition is accumulating sufficient evidence to reach a general conclusion based on the highest degree of probability attainable.

Although this may leave room for error inversely proportional to the reliability of the evidence, it is the closest we can come to absolute truth outside of mathematics, self-evident and self-defining first principles, or first-person knowledge.

As mentioned earlier, we must recognize that there are people who have such dogged personal beliefs that no amount of truth or reality or any level of probability would convince them to accept the proof provided by any amount of reliable, objective evidence. They literally do not want to be bothered with the facts. We must understand that in order for proof to be persuasive, the will must cooperate with the mind. Thus we can make the observation that persons of goodwill who are seeking the truth will be persuaded by good reasoning.

## Summary

We established that almost all our daily decisions are made based on the probability of truth, not on absolute truth, and that the will must cooperate with the mind. If our rational mind accepts truth based on the evidence but our will chooses to ignore it or even reject it outright, we might just as well kiss reality goodbye and continue to live in a world of make-believe! The acceptance of truth is volitional; we can, and many do, reject it. We cannot wake a person who is only pretending to be asleep.

# Chapter 10

# A Basic Law of Physics

## The Laws of Thermodynamics

A basic understanding of some laws of physics will help us in our discussion of belief systems. We are all aware of the accepted truth that matter cannot be created or destroyed, only changed.

Around 1797, Count Rumford was intrigued by this changing of matter, more particularly in the transfer of energy. His studies led him to discover that mechanical energy could generate large amounts of heat. The establishment, formulation, and universal acceptance of the laws that arose from the study of the transfer of energy came to be known as the laws of thermodynamics.

During the industrial revolution, staggering amounts of money (by the standards of that period) were poured into this research with the hope of discovering an engine that could produce more output (energy) than it consumed. Although no such engine was ever conceived, the research provided invaluable data in the physical sciences. Research into the transfer or conversion of energy established that energy (absent any outside interference) would transfer only from a hotter area to a cooler area, never in the opposite direction, and that in the process, entropy would increase (the rate of decay would accelerate; that is, the usefulness of the energy available for conversion to mechanical work would decrease).

Further study showed that the closer this heat transfer occurred to absolute zero, the slower the entropy would occur, until theoretically, at absolute zero, entropy would cease and no further conversion would be possible.

By 1873, Joseph W. Gibbs had clearly formulated the first two laws. We now accept that there are three laws; here are very brief definitions.

- First Law of Thermodynamics: Energy can be transferred into many forms but cannot be created or destroyed. Thus the total amount of energy in the universe is constant.
- Second Law of Thermodynamics: Heat (energy) always transfers from hot to cold, and the entropy (decay) of an isolated system always increases with time. Thus within a closed universe, energy and matter are becoming less useful as time goes on. The amount of useful energy available for conversion (work) is constantly decreasing as time goes on.
- Third Law of Thermodynamics: If all the energy could be removed from molecules, a state called absolute zero would occur: −273.15 Celsius!

## The Law of Causality

Science has on the whole accepted that things do not just pop into existence. If they did, the universe would be chaotic. The imagination runs rampant with scenarios of things just popping into existence. Therefore, the acceptance of the law of causality: everything that comes to be has a cause.

## The Universe from Nothing—Quantum Physics

Quantum physics is the study of subatomic phenomena. Self-proclaimed atheist and professor of cosmology Lawrence Krauss, of Arizona State University, recently caused a big stir with his book *The Universe from Nothing*.

He wrote that while it is true that to be, everything has to have a cause, what happens at the quantum level dispenses with the need for a cause, such as a god. Quantum mechanics shows that something can come from nothing; in fact, he states that in quantum mechanics, nothing always turns into something. The reason for this is that "nothing" is highly unstable and will become "something."

While this is very intriguing, further inquiry shows there is a problem with definitions. When we explore the meaning of "nothing," we expect to have it defined as "no thing." An analysis of Krauss's book shows that some of the quantum vacuum fields in question contained fluctuating energy from which particles popped into and out of existence.

In his book *Quantum Mechanics*, David Albert, a professor of theoretical physics and also an atheist, questioned Krauss's logic rather emphatically by stating that Krauss's quantum vacuum fields often started with "something." Some arrangements of his quantum fields had a quantum vacuum with energy fields while others didn't. The ones that did produced something; the ones that didn't produced nothing. To emphasize his point, he wrote that it would be like saying a hand clinched into a fist had no fingers, then the fingers miraculously appear when the hand slowly unclenches.

It is reported that Krauss rejected Albert's criticism and questioned his philosophical prowess. Krauss made it clear that he preferred his own definition of "nothing."

## Summary

These laws of thermodynamics represent scientific proof that matter cannot be created nor destroyed, thus showing that energy/matter in the universe is constant. Furthermore, this research shows that undisturbed, the transfer of energy goes only from hot to cold with an increasing rate of decay. In time, this means that the universe will reach a state or near state of equilibrium resulting in no further transfer of energy, hence death.

Note the word *undisturbed* above. Do we believe there is any power on earth that could change (disturb) the ongoing processes in the universe?

Taking this law to its logical next step proves to us that energy/matter tends toward decay. We experience this in our daily lives; our bodies as well as our homes require constant maintenance or they quickly deteriorate, and our vehicles tend to rust and fall apart without maintenance, and so on.

The law of causality has on the whole been universally accepted. The disparity comes in determining the cause. The atheist maintains that the cause was pure happenstance and an accident.

The palpable excitement of the atheistic community when Krauss released his quantum physics "findings" has all but disappeared. I included it in this presentation because occasionally, someone will bring it up as the ultimate proof of the true creation of the universe.

## Review of Part 2

Answers to the following questions will help you understand the material presented.

1. What is a worldview?
2. Define the components of a worldview.
3. Define the correspondence theory of truth.
4. What is the theory known as first principles?
5. Name two of the three instances when we can reasonably expect to attain absolute truth.
6. Most of our daily decisions are made on the probability that the information available to us is true. Name at least three factors that will help us improve the probability of truth.
7. Explain the following statement: "Proof for any worldview within the areas of knowledge specified cannot rise above rational probability."
8. Define the logical law of noncontradiction.
9. In the logical law of inference, do you have to prove the conclusion? Explain your answer.
10. Based on the law of thermodynamics, will the universe last forever? Why?
11. A recent book by Krauss on quantum physics purported to prove that you could create something from nothing, thus negating the need for a creator. Did the book achieve its claim? Why or why not?
12. What do we mean by the statement "The will must cooperate with the mind"?

We now move on to part 3, in which we will review some of the major belief systems. As you go through the different belief systems, try to remember the tests we have discussed and see how they might apply.

*Part 3:*

# Belief Systems

# Overview of Part 3

The world's religions include a wide range of beliefs. To try to make this discussion meaningful, I will combine all religions into belief systems, each of which will include all religions with similar beliefs. We will try to ascertain which belief system or religion provides the most meaningful answers to our three basic questions:

> Where did I come from?
> What am I doing here?
> What happens to me after I die?

It is not within the parameters of this discussion to provide or even attempt to provide complete dissertations on each religion discussed; instead, I will provide overviews that supply enough information to show the major differences among them. I hope you will be challenged and interested enough to continue more in-depth research to expand your knowledge.

## Background on Religious Beliefs

For some 1,400 years, from when Emperor Constantine decreed that Christianity was the Roman Empire's state religion until the midnineteenth century, Christianity was the major religious influence in the Western world. The Western world's laws, moral standards, ethics, and general worldviews were for the most part based on Christian principles and beliefs.

The Reformation in the sixteenth century, the initiation of the Enlightenment in the eighteenth century, and the start of naturalism with the publication of Darwin's *On the Origin of Species* in the midnineteenth century led to a plethora of differing worldviews and religions.

## The Different Belief Systems

In our review of belief systems, we will be severely handicapped by the enormity of the task. In the United States alone there are thousands of registered religions. Therefore, it would be wise to review the definition of two key terms. A *belief system* is used to indicate large groups of people that for the most part have similar beliefs. *Religion* is used to indicate subgroups within a belief system that have some differences within their group.

The major belief systems (worldviews) that we will look at include

- Atheism—no god
- Pantheism—many gods
- Monotheism—one God

In our review of the various belief systems, we will discuss each system's beliefs in certain critical areas that will help us understand and provide a common base for analytic comparison. We need to know what each belief system thinks about

1. God
2. creation
3. morals/ethics
4. suffering and evil
5. salvation (eternal life)
6. death and the afterlife
7. the belief system's claims to truth

Once we understand each belief system's worldviews on each of these seven areas, we will be in a better position to draw rational comparisons.

**Adherents to Major World Religions**

To help us gain perspective, we include the following information, acknowledging studies that attempt to show the size of the major religions are always suspect because of the great diversity and classification problems mentioned above. With this caveat and only for informational purposes, we include the results of a worldwide survey completed in 1994 [worldwide population at the time approximately 6 billion] of some of the better-known religions.

- Christianity—33 percent (2.1 billion)
- Islam—21 percent (1.5 billion)
- Nonreligious—16 percent (1.1 billion)
- Hinduism—14 percent (0.9 billion)
- Chinese traditional—6 percent (0.39 billion)
- Buddhism—6 percent (0.38 billion)
- Judaism—0.2 percent (14 million)[2]

After our discussion of these belief systems, we will compare them with the tools discussed in part 2.

---

[2]    These statistics were posted in 2005 by Adherents.com.

# Chapter 11

# Atheism—There Is No God

Atheism (from the Greek *atheo*, godless) is the philosophical foundation for several nonbelieving groups, including atheists, naturalists, and secular humanists. Atheism is also believed to have given birth to the modernists, who incorporated some of the more traditional belief systems in their worldview.

Atheism believes that there is no truth beyond the five senses and that there is nothing beyond the material universe. Its doctrine is that scientific laws are adequate to account for all phenomena. The universe is eternal and has always existed; there is no creator. This belief of eternality lasted for over 2,500 years and has, for the most part, been replaced by the big bang theory.

This belief system is also foundational for secular humanism, a philosophy that rejects supernaturalism and stresses an individual's dignity and worth and capacity for self-realization through reason. Secular humanism has become very prevalent in Western culture.

Secular humanists adopted their Humanist Manifesto I in 1933 and published their Humanist Manifesto II in 1973. Theses manifestos outlined their beliefs. Signatories to these manifestos and adherents to this belief system include national leaders with full access to and in many cases control of the media, universities, businesses, and significant segments of our government.

To enable us to better understand this very large and complex topic, we will look at and compare common points in each belief system. These points have been mentioned earlier.

## God

According to atheists, there is no god. Reality consists only of matter; there is nothing but nature, and everything has a natural explanation. All that exists is physical; there is no supernatural realm; humans are only physical beings with no soul or spirit. People are the crowning achievement of the evolutionary process; they are totally self-aware and fully capable of ethical behavior. All knowledge is within people's grasp; they control their destinies and ethics and are self-sufficient. Humanity is the measure of all things.

## Creation

The universe has always existed; no, it was created as a result of a big bang! [A big bang of what?] There is no need for a creator. "The universe is self-existing and not created" (Humanist Manifesto I).

Humans evolved, and like the universe, they operate like machines. Everything humans are or do can be reduced to physical or chemical processes; even their thoughts are simply chemical or neurological impulses. Nonetheless, they are somehow separated from the rest of the animals by their "elevated" level of existence [how they were elevated or what elevated them is yet to be determined].

## Morals and Ethics

There is no moral absolute or standard of right or wrong. Moral values derive their source from human experience. Ethics arise from human need and interest and are relative. Past puritanical beliefs and cultures unduly repressed sexual conduct. "Short of harming others ... individuals should be permitted to express their sexual proclivities and lifestyles as they desire" (Humanist Manifesto II).

Ethics are relative because they are a projection of humans' subjective feelings. If there is any instinctive repulsion of certain acts such as murder, it is because the process of evolution programmed [does matter have the ability to program?] that in people.

## Suffering and Evil

Suffering and pain are real, but we have or can acquire the means to take care of ourselves. But, to naturalists, suffering and pain are to be expected because survival of the fittest requires the elimination of the weak; this elimination process can of necessity be painful. Sin and evil are nonstarters since to have sin, we have to have a right and wrong, and of course that is relative. Sin and evil can be seen as the same as the struggle in the survival of the fittest in which people are striving to dominate others by any means possible. In this context, the naturalist cannot see sin as evil. "We are responsible for what we are or will be" (Humanist Manifesto II).

## Salvation

There is no salvation. Other than our inexplicably elevated status over other earthly creatures, there is no difference between us and them. We are material creatures; there is nothing to be saved from or to. "Religious Humanism considers the complete realization of human personality to be the end of man's life" (Humanist Manifesto II).

## Death and the Afterlife

There is no afterlife. Once we die, there is nothing to pass on to, no soul to live on, no afterlife; we go to the grave and are no more. We do not even merge and become one with the universal god pantheists believe in. Secular humanists subscribe to the belief that "individuals have the right to suicide." "There is no credible evidence that life survives the death of the body. We continue to exist in our progeny and in the way that our lives influenced others" (Humanist Manifesto II). Therefore, the only way we can continue to "live" is through our children. If we have no children, it's the end of the line for us. Many so-called committed naturalists and atheists have a real problem with this doctrine. Their instincts tell them there has to be something else; presumably, these are the people who evolved into modernists then postmodernists.

**Claim to Truth**

Atheists and naturalists depend almost entirely on science for their "truth." "If I can't see it, touch it, or feel it, it doesn't exist."

**Summary**

Science by definition has to involve truth and certainty. When scientific proof is demanded, it is understood that this proof is a product of the truth and is derived from testing, observation, and the ability to retest (repeatability) and to each time get the same results.

When classical science departs into areas that cannot be tested or observed, problems arise. History cannot be tested nor observed since by definition it is in the past. Other disciplines are also problematic for scientific testing.

Secular humanists believe "the way to determine the existence and value of any and all realities is by means of intelligent inquiry and by the assessment of their relation to human needs ... in light of scientific spirit and method" (Humanist Manifesto I). Therefore, if "reality" i.e., "truth," is based on human needs, truth becomes relative.

Common sense and our human experience show, therefore, that all truth cannot depend on classical science for verifiability. I say classical science because the term *scientific method* can and is often used to define tried-and-true methods that do not involve actual laboratory testing. Examples when the term *scientific method* could be used include any testing using the laws of logic and the support of truth through probability.

We must remember that scientific research and studies can only provide data. The interpretation of that data is a function of the discipline of philosophy whether conducted by a philosopher, doctor, scientist, or anybody else. Science provides data; philosophy interprets it.

A final word: to be a true atheist, you have no option but to believe that humanity is merely a fortunate cosmic accident brought about by a lucky arrangement of molecules, a chemical equation, an evolved slime pool, and an animal that has learned to wear clothes.

# Chapter 12

# Pantheism—There Are Many Gods

Pantheism comes from the Greek *pan* (all) and *theos* (god); literally, "all is god." According to *Merriam-Webster*, it is "a doctrine that equates god with the forces and laws of the universe." This basic theological concept originated in the East, and a number of the world's well-known religions subscribe to its main concepts. Adherents to the concept of multiple gods include those who practice

- Hinduism, also well known for its belief in reincarnation
- Zen Buddhism, a variation of Buddhism. Generally, Buddhism does not worship a deity but is more a lifestyle.
- Taoism, generally practiced in China
- Christian Science
- The Unity Church
- Scientology
- Polytheism
- New Age, among others.

Animism probably should be included in this category. Animism attributes a soul or spirit to almost everything animate and inanimate. Native Americans paid homage and respect to the tree spirit, the great mountain spirit, and so on.

Some would include Mormonism in this category because of its belief that Jesus was born as a result of a union between a god and a goddess and its concept that Mormon men if faithful and in good standing when they die, will inherit their own worlds they will rule over as gods.

**God**

All reality (the universe and everything in it) is god. If anything that is not god appears to exist, it is *maya* (illusion) and really does not exist. God has no personality and can best be described as an it. It has no relationship with people and does not intervene in their affairs. Since everything is god and we are a part of everything, we too are god.

Pantheists often use contradiction or paradoxical thinking in what they think will bring devotees to a higher level of awareness, thus closer to the universal god. For example, Zen Buddhism asks, "What is the sound of one hand clapping?" The Brahman [the soul of god] Hindus claim is "always and never." [Presumably the soul of god has "always existed" and "never existed"].

Hindus identify the human soul as atman and the soul of god as Brahman. We should spend our time focusing in uniting our atman with the Brahman by meditating and purging our bodies of earthly cravings. There is no need to worry about human needs or welfare since all pain, suffering, and material things are maya.

**Creation**

While some forms of pantheism maintain that a created physical universe is an illusion because only god exists, all agree that the physical world is inseparable from god.

**Morals and Ethics**

Most pantheists teach that we should live moral lives, although there is no basis for determining morality.

## Suffering and Evil

Since god is everything spiritual and physical and since it has no feelings, suffering is an illusion. God is not a moral being, so once you become one with god, you move beyond good and evil.

## Salvation

Salvation consists in becoming one with God; we move from the illusion of this life to oneness with god through meditation, incantations, hallucinatory agents, or other techniques that alter our consciousness to a level that brings us closer to the universal god.

Many pantheists also believe in the law of karma, the idea that we must be reincarnated after death to return to our next life in a state dictated by the severity of our sins in the life just departed [which begs the question, if there is no basis for morality, how do we determine what sin is?]. The greater our sin in the past life, the lower the life form we return to. This might explain why in some Eastern Hindu nations, dogs are often beaten, presumably to punish the sinner for his or her past sins. Reincarnation will continue until our karma improves to a level that frees us from this cycle to a level of consciousness that allows us to unite with the universal god.

## Death and the Afterlife

In the pantheistic belief, everyone will eventually reach oneness with God. The individual soul will be absorbed into the soul of God with no identity. People will cease to be individuals with specific identities.

## Claim to Truth

The Vedas, a collection of hymns, prayers, and some liturgical formulas, are believed to have been written 700–800 BC. They are the earliest known ancient Hindu writings. Otherwise, pantheism has no verifiable historical basis for its beliefs; its truth claims are unverifiable, so they must be taken totally on faith.

Classification of the various belief systems is at best difficult and can sometimes result in rather odd bedfellows. The following worldviews can be said to be spin offs of secular humanism but are included in the pantheistic category because they are not as definitive about their god or gods or lack thereof as are atheists or theists. So the following would best describe the more modernistic thought: God is … whatever.

## *Modernism*

*Merriam-Webster* defines modernism as "a tendency in theology to accommodate traditional religious teaching to contemporary thought and especially to devalue supernatural elements." As mentioned, in secular humanism, there is no god other than man. This left the spiritual void in humanity unfilled.

To compensate, a segment of secular humanists and others began to accommodate some traditional religious beliefs they felt were reasonable and fit the spectrum of modern thought. Modern thought excluded all things supernatural. This new accommodation of some secular humanism, a bit of naturalism with a sprinkling of traditional religion, became known as modernism. Nonetheless, modernists generally accepted that truth was rational and adhered to fundamental laws of logic … well, kind of.

## *Postmodernism*

This rapidly expanding belief system moves further away from secular humanism and breaks from modernism because it rejects people's ability to reason their way to truth because there is no objective truth. Truth is subjective and comes from human ideas and experiences as we interpret them through our culture.

Postmodernists believe people are products of their cultures, which create their attitudes and thought processes. Thus, the way they think is not only influenced by their culture, it is also determined by their culture.

Therefore, there is no objective, absolute, or universal truth because all truth is relative and is a product of cultural beliefs. Since all cultures differ, there is no single truth applicable to everyone.

The outcome of this belief system completely removes all ability to judge religious, ethical, or social behavior of any culture because one culture's reality is not compatible with another's; all belief systems are equally true.

Postmodernists believe truth and language heavily influence each other because people think in words and these words are different in different cultures. If we *say* the right words, we will then *think* the correct things.

This belief has given rise to politically correct speech, which most people presuppose was intended to make us more aware of and teach us to be more sensitive to other people's feelings. In reality, politically correct speech is intended to change people by changing their cultural environments. Thus, by changing the way people talk, you can change society.

We must be aware that as the postmodernist movement continues to grow, as its influence in our universities, government, and even our churches expands, it will have an increasing propensity to manipulate and construct reality. Once this happens, we will have established a social-political agenda at a very high price, the sacrifice of truth.

We must ask ourselves, is it morally or intellectually responsible to sacrifice truth for such concepts as openness and tolerance? Let's be mindful of the political correctness we experience or see and hear in the media and assess it intelligently.

## Summary

Postmodernism can be traced to the midtwentieth century. It has grown very rapidly and has influenced most areas of our society. It is taught in our universities, dominates our entertainment industry, has infiltrated most of our political thinking, has practically taken control of our news media, and has made significant inroads into many of our churches.

.    Relativism and pluralism are at the core of postmodernism, yet its adherents often have trouble living by its guidance. Few postmodernists believe the lifestyle of criminals, who are doing nothing more than living by their codes of conduct, should be tolerated; few of them accept the portion of certain sects of Hinduism that dictate the burning alive of a late husband's widow on his funeral pyre. Carried to the extreme, they would not have been able to judge much less criticize Adolph Hitler's atrocities against the Jews. They would have had to "tolerate" it.

In a society so entrenched in postmodernism, why are there so many lawsuits filed in the United States? Relativism does mean that we should not judge what others do, right? Tolerance is a mainstay of postmodernism, yet there is no tolerance in our schools for the teaching of Creation. There is no tolerance for the belief that the killing of an unborn child is the killing of another human being. If your views do not concur with theirs, you are ostracized, not tolerated.

Addressing their absolute claim that there is no absolute truth, Dennis McCallum in his *The Death of Truth* said it best: "Postmodern preachers declare that if we find anyone claiming to know truth, that person we should ignore. By their own test they should be ignored!" because they used an absolute statement in their argument!

A final word must include the point that the outcome of full acceptance of relativism and complete tolerance would undoubtedly lead to total moral anarchy.

# Chapter 13

# Monotheism—There Is One God

The word *monotheism* comes from the Greek *mono* (one) and *theos* (God). The religions we will discuss in this category all believe there is only one God. The two major world religions in terms of numbers of professed adherents are Christianity (approximately 33 percent of the world's population) and Islam (with approximately 21 percent).

A third world religion falls in this category, though its adherents are relatively few in number, 0.2 percent of the world's population, of which just under half live in the United States. It has had a major impact in our world for some four thousand years. Because of its huge impact, I will include it in this discussion. This third religion is of course Judaism.

All three religions accept at least part of the Old Testament of the Christian Bible as their own. A word of caution: although all three religions claim a commonality of lineage through Abraham (approximately 2100 BC), the interpretation and sequence of events varies to some degree between Islam and the other two. With a few rather significant exceptions, Judaism and Christianity accept and interpret the Old Testament in the same way.

Islam accepts the first five books of the Bible as its own. These books are known as the Torah or the Pentateuch, with Moses accepted as the author. These books are also known as the Law Books. Some Islamic sects believe some or all of these five books have been corrupted. All Islam believes the rest of the Bible has been corrupted and superseded by the Qur'an.

Islam traces its ancestry up to Abraham through Abraham's son by Hagar, Abraham's wife's maidservant. The son's name was Ishmael. When Hagar was pregnant, Sarah, Abraham's wife, began to despise and mistreat her.

Hagar fled and while fleeing an angel appeared to Hagar and told her she would give birth to a son ... she would name him Ishmael ... he would be a wild donkey of a man ... whose hand would be against everyone ... and everyone's hand against him ... he would live in hostility toward all his brothers. Hagar returned to Sarah and bore the son. Abraham was then 86 years old. (Genesis 16:11–16)

Judaism and Christianity trace their lineage up to Abraham through Isaac, his son by his wife Sarah. Ishmael was fourteen and Abraham was a hundred when Isaac was born. The first five in the Jewish/Christian lineage down from and including Abraham were Abraham, Isaac, Jacob, Judah, and Perez.

After Isaac was born, Sarah was distressed and told Abraham to get rid of the slave woman and her son. After being assured by God that as his offspring, Ishmael would be made into a nation, Abraham, after providing food and water, reluctantly sent her and her son on their way.

We can see that in spite of their distant familial relationship, from the beginning, the relationship between Jews and Muslims has been somewhat less than stellar.

## Islam

The word *islam* means "surrender" or "submission." A Muslim is one who submits to Allah and is an adherent of Islam. Muhammad is Allah's final prophet; he was preceded by several others, including Noah, Abraham, Moses, David, and Jesus. The prophets before Muhammad were great prophets who brought God's message to the people and wrote these revelations from God into the Old and New Testaments. In Islam, Jesus is a prophet, not God.

Muhammad was born in Mecca (now part of Saudi Arabia) in AD 570 into a family that ruled their tribe. He grew up in tribes that were constantly at war and became quite a warrior himself. While he was growing up, the Arabs worshipped some 360 gods, one for each day of the lunar year. His favorite god was Allah, the moon god.

Muhammad often sought solitude, and, when he was around thirty-five, while meditating in a cave, the angel Gabriel appeared to him and brought recitations from God that Muhammad memorized because he could neither read nor write. He later passed these sayings to his friends who wrote them down. Many years later, the fourth leader of Islam, Caliph Uthman, gathered these writings and disseminated them as the Qur'an.

Muslims consider the Qur'an the divine word of Allah while considering the Bible (with the exception of the first five books) corrupt. Authoritatively, the Hadith, a collection of Muhammad's sayings and deeds as recorded by his companions, is second only to the Qur'an.

Muhammad started spreading his new religion, choosing Allah as the only god, by all means possible to convert people. One of his claims was that Allah commanded him to fight people until they became Muslims.

Increasing opposition to his tactics and new religion from his contemporaries in Mecca led him to move to Medina in AD 620, where his religion grew in converts and power. In 631, he returned to Mecca and eliminated all opposition by conversion or the sword.

He died in 632 after choosing Abu Bakr, his favorite wife's father, as his successor.

Abu Bakr became the caliph of the Islamic sect known as the Sunnis, who represent about 90 percent of the Islamic world. The majority of the Sunnis live in Asia. The Sunnis believe that the Qur'an is their only tie to Allah. Sunnis believe that Muhammad's gifts died with him.

After Muhammad died, some Islamic leaders felt that Muhammad's son-in-law Ali had received some of the prophet's spirituality and appointed him as their leader, the imam. To this date, imams lead the Islamic sect known as the Shi'ites; they represent most of the remaining Islamic population.

There are several other minor sects, among them the Sufi and possibly the Nation of Islam [NOI, Louis Farrakhan's group], though historically, the Muslims have not fully accepted the NOI.

Because of their spiritual lineage, Shi'ites believe that the imam's authority is on a par with the Qur'an. Geographically, present-day Shi'ites occupy the areas of Saudi Arabia, Iraq, Syria, Iran, Yemen, and Lebanon. The Shi'ites await the coming of the twelfth imam, also known as the *Madhi.*

Imam Hasan Al-Askari, the eleventh imam, bore a son in the thirteenth century. When the son was five, ongoing conflicts caused him to go into hiding in caves.

Shi'ites believe that sometime in the near future, when the world is experiencing three years of horrendous chaos, tyranny, and oppression, and just before the judgment day, the twelfth imam, Madhi, will supernaturally reappear and rule over all the Arabs and the entire world under *shari'ah* law for seven years, eradicating all tyranny and oppression and bringing harmony and peace.

Iran's Ahmadinejad claimed he was directed by Allah to prepare the way for the twelfth imam, and Ahmadinejad's successor has not refuted this claim. For the Madhi to save the world, the world must first be thrown into chaos and subjugation. A nuclear Iran?

Let's turn our discussion to the comparative criteria we've established.

## God

There is only one Allah, the Arabic word for God; all other gods are false. When people say that Allah and God are one and the same, they are technically correct. However, what Allah is to a Muslim and what God is to a Christian are worlds apart. Allah expects works, and he wants converts by the sword if necessary. Allah sees all things, is everywhere, and is all powerful. Allah is in complete control of everything and ordains everything that occurs. Angels exist and are created from light. The jinn are another race of beings created from fire; they are invisible and are all around us.

## Creation

Allah is the creator and sustainer of the universe. He created the heavens and the earth. Man is made from the dust of the earth.

## Morals and Ethics

Of the many sins, one of the greatest is *shirk*, that is, attributing partners to Allah. To say that Allah is a trinity would be shirk, an unforgivable sin. Another sin punishable by death is for a Muslim to leave Islam. Gambling and drinking alcohol are major sins.

## Suffering and Evil

There is real suffering, but suffering and even dying for Allah is good.

### Salvation

Muhammad called his people to repent from idol worship, to do good, to serve Allah, and on that day of judgment, man's works would be weighed. A Muslim who fulfills the five pillars of Islam remains faithful to Islam and repents of sin will, by Allah's grace, make it to *jannah* (paradise). Briefly, the five pillars are

- *shahada*: The proclamation that "There is no true God except Allah and Muhammad is the messenger of Allah."
- *salat*: Prayer five times a day, the first at dawn and the last at sunset.
- *saum*: Fasting. To deny his own needs and seek Allah, a Muslim will forgo eating, drinking, or sexual relations during daylight hours for the entire month of Ramadan.
- *zakat*: Almsgiving.
- *haji*: Pilgrimage, if able, to Mecca during the first half of the last month of the lunar year.

### Death and the Afterlife

Those whose good deeds outweighed their bad deeds might, by Allah's grace, be saved and enter paradise. There is no allowance for deathbed conversions. The unsaved, which includes all non-Muslims, go to hell, a place of fire and boiling water. Paradise, on the other hand, is a garden of bliss and fruit with rivers, lots of carpets and cushions, and maidens pure and holy.

### Islam's Claims to Truth

Caliph Uthman, the fourth caliph after Muhammad, gathered all the fragments of the Qur'anic writings and assembled, approved, and disseminated the Qur'an throughout the Muslim world. Muslims consider the Hadith second only to the Qur'an. The Hadith is a collection of sayings and deeds of Muhammad and are considered authoritative and instructive. The Hadith supplements the Qur'an.

## Summary of Islam

Islam is one of the world's fastest-growing religions; it attracts converts by all means possible, including the word and the sword. The ultimate worldly goal of the Muslims is shari'ah law throughout the world. This would put everyone under its rule.

## Judaism

Judaism (Hebrew *Yehudah*, "Judah") is a religion and a nation/ culture. Judah is the name of one of the twelve sons of Jacob, grandson of Abraham, the founding father of the chosen people, the Israelites.

Specifically, Judaism traces its lineage to the covenant God made with Abraham that made him and his descendants a nation of priests, a chosen people, and promised them a land of milk and honey. This land was then called Canaan and is now Israel and the surrounding area. It is estimated that present Israel occupies less than a quarter of the original promised land.

Abraham, Isaac, and Jacob (God changed Jacob's name to Israel) were the patriarchs of Judaism. Joseph, son of Jacob, was second only to Pharaoh in Egypt. During a time of famine, he brought all his family to Egypt. During their four hundred years in Egypt, their numbers rapidly increased and they went from people that were welcomed to people who were slaves.

God selected Moses to lead them out of Egypt. During their forty years' wandering through the desert on their way to the promised land, God gave Moses his law, which included the Ten Commandments and in time other laws we now call the Mosaic Law.

Moses is considered the author of the first five books of the Old Testament, known as the Torah. The Talmud and Midrash are rabbinic, legal, and narrative interpretations of the Torah and are considered sacred.

Over the next 1,500 years, until the birth of Jesus, Jews went through many periods of feast and famine, cycles of worshipping God and worshipping false gods. These periods culminated with their defeat and enslavement by the Babylonians about 600 BC.

After some seventy years of enslavement, they returned to Judah (Israel) and rebuilt their homeland. However, their cyclical bouts with God continued until their defeat by the Romans. Although they continued to live in their lands, they were under Roman subjugation when Christ was born in Bethlehem about 3 BC.

Jews never accepted Christ as their Messiah and believe their Messiah is yet to come. After a major Jewish uprising in AD 70, the Romans soundly defeated them and destroyed or plundered everything Jewish, including their center of worship, the temple (which to this day has yet to be rebuilt). Since that defeat, the Jews were without a homeland until the establishment of Israel as a nation in 1948.

The Jewish people have been survivors; they have endured Egyptian and Babylonian enslavement and the near annihilation and destruction of their cities and their center of worship by the Romans.

They endured the Inquisition, expulsion from England in 1290 to approximately 1650, expulsion from France in 1306 and 1394 to approximately 1789, and expulsion from Spain and Portugal in 1492. After all this, they had to endure Hitler's murdering of millions of them in his attempt to rid the world of Zionists. More recently, they endured several Arab-led wars since their reestablishment as a nation in 1948.

For a group of people with less than 0.2 percent of the world's population, they have made a major impact on the world for some four thousand years. They have won some forty percent of all the Pulitzer prizes, they manage or otherwise control a large segment of the world's financial resources, and they are mentioned in some 20 percent of world news. They continue to be at the center of the world's attention.

Moving on to the comparative criteria.

## God

There is only one God. Jesus was a prophet but not God. The Davidic (from the throne of King David) Messiah who will eventually lead Israel back to its glory is still awaited.

## Creation

Orthodox Jews hold to the creation as depicted in the books of Moses. God created the heavens, the earth, and everything therein. Man was created from the dust of the earth, and woman was created from man's rib.

## Morals and Ethics

Conscience is the pain of the human spirit. In a rabbinical perspective, sin is a rejection of God's will. Those who cause others to sin are worse than those who kill others because murderers exclude only their victims from this life, while those who cause others to sin exclude them from the world to come. Reformed Judaism believes that sin is caused by the evil inclination in man, which drives him to gratify his instincts and ambitions.

## Suffering and Evil

Some modern Jewish philosophers say that man is not evil by nature but that his misuse of nature generates evil. By being disobedient to God's command, humanity was ejected from the luxuriant and bountiful garden of Eden and thrust into working hard— tilling the soil and fighting thorns and rocks—to eke out an existence. Wives were to be obedient to their husbands and go through the painful process of giving birth. The Jewish people are indeed cognizant of suffering.

## Salvation

"They asked of wisdom, 'What is the punishment of the sinner?' Wisdom replied: 'Evil pursueth sinners.' They asked of prophecy, 'What is the punishment of sinners?' Prophecy replied, 'The soul that sinneth it shall die.' Then they asked of the Holy One, blessed be He, 'What is the punishment of the sinner?' He replied: 'Let him repent and he will find atonement.'" If you repent of your sins and follow God's laws, you will find salvation.

## Death and the Afterlife

Orthodox Judaism maintains a belief in the future resurrection of the dead as part of God's redemption. It also believes in the immortality of the soul after death. Reformed Judaism no longer believes in the resurrection of the dead, but it does maintain the belief of spiritual life after death.

## Judaism's Claims to Truth

The Tanakh (Old Testament Bible) is divided into three segments.

- The Torah: The first five books of the Old Testament.
- The Nevi'im: The books written by the prophets.
- The Ketuvim: The rest of the Old Testament, also known as the Writings.

In addition to the Tanakh, Jewish believers have two other sacred books, the Talmud and the Oral Law. Rabbinic laws and lore are included in the Talmud. The Torah, with its 613 commandments, is also called the written law. The Oral Law is a legal commentary on the Torah and is a very explicit guide to its 613 laws and commandments.

Judaism has no shortage of ancient writings and secular historical proofs supporting its beliefs.

## Summary of Judaism

One of God's greatest miracles has been the survival of the Jews. From their Abrahamic inception some four thousand years ago to the present, there are no people that have lived so long, been rejected so much, been persecuted almost continuously, been enslaved twice, subjugated countless times, ejected from their country twice, almost annihilated several times, yet were reborn as a nation and succeeded immeasurably against all odds. They continues to thwart those who would wish them ill.

A story has circulated for centuries about a very powerful king who had converted to Christianity. On his deathbed, one of his subjects asked him how he came to believe that God was real. It is reported that he said, "I can do that in three short words, 'the Jewish people.'"

## Christianity[3]

The word *Christ* comes from the Hebrew word for Messiah, while the word *Christian* was first used in Antioch around AD 37/38 to describe the followers of Christ. Prior to this time, they were simply called people of "the Way," presumably because they claimed to know the way to salvation.

The Jewish Tanakh (Old Testament) is replete with prophecies about the coming Messiah. Rabbinical belief had him coming as a warrior king to free them from the bondage of Rome and to reinstate the glory days of Israel.

Jesus was born in Bethlehem about 3 BC of Jewish parents. At that time, Israel had been under Roman subjugation for many years. After surviving an attempt by King Herod, a Roman appointee, to kill him shortly after his birth (having heard a new Jewish king had been born in Bethlehem, Herod considered him a future threat), his family moved to Egypt. After King Herod's death, they moved back to Judea and settled in Nazareth, where he picked up his father's carpentry trade.

Other than a reference of his family's trip to Jerusalem when Jesus was twelve, he was not heard from again until his baptism, prior to the start of his ministry, when he was thirty. Christianity's start goes back to this ministry.

Shortly after the start of his ministry, he began selecting men to train and help him spread the word. These twelve men (known as the original apostles) believed in and accepted him as the long-awaited Jewish Messiah. Jesus preached a gospel of love, service, and humility while performing countless healings and other miracles. His interpretations of the Mosaic Law were in many cases very different from rabbinical interpretations.

During the three years of his ministry, he became very popular and attracted large crowds wherever he preached. This was in stark

---

[3] Note that all references to Christian belief and doctrine are strictly biblical.

contrast to the feelings of the established religious leaders who had become very concerned about his popularity and the new religion he was spreading. These leaders had already decided that Jesus could not have been the long-awaited Messiah because his message was all wrong and he was obviously not the warrior king they had anticipated. They thought his message of love, service, and humility certainly was not the way to free Israel and restore it to its former grandeur.

Jesus maintained that the establishment leaders had become more interested in the law and the minutiae of the law than they were in worshipping God and bringing in new followers to God. This greatly infuriated the religious leaders, who began looking for a way to silence him. The opportunity presented itself when Jesus claimed he was the son of God. The Sanhedrin (religious leaders) put him on trial for blasphemy, convicted him, turned him over to Pontius Pilate, and convinced Pilate to have Jesus crucified.

Jesus was crucified and buried, and on the third day, he was resurrected. He appeared in the flesh to the apostles (eleven at that point since Judas Iscariot had committed suicide), other disciples who had followed him, some of the women who had supported his ministry, and some five hundred of his followers. He continued to train and instruct his apostles and disciples for forty days, after which he ascended into heaven.

Christianity grew very rapidly in the first century. In the second and third centuries, persecutions against Christians reached new heights with thousands of Christians being martyred, often savagely.

In the fourth century, Emperor Constantine converted to Christianity and made it the official religion of Rome. This of course led to the cessation of persecutions and even more-rapid growth. With this growth, tensions between the Eastern and Western churches (which had differences on the use of icons, the Holy Spirit, and Easter) were becoming apparent. This came to a head in 1054, when Pope Leo IX excommunicated the patriarch of Constantinople, leader of the Eastern Church. The patriarch condemned the pope in return. Ever since, the rift between the Roman Catholic Church and the Greek Orthodox Church has existed. As I write this, there are some ongoing attempts at reconciliation.

The sixteenth century was the time of the Reformation, when certain groups of Christians led by a German monk, Martin Luther, thought the church had drifted from biblical guidance and doctrine and sought to bring the church back to basic biblical worship. The Reformation gave rise to the third major Christian group in the religion now known as the Protestants. In spite of these splits, the overall Christian community continued to grow to become the largest religious group in the world.

Now to the comparative criteria.

## God

Christians believe that there is only one God. However, Christians are the only religion that believes in the Trinity, that is, one God in three persons: God the Father, God the Son, and God the Holy Spirit. God is omniscient (knows everything), omnipotent (is all powerful), omnipresent (is everywhere), and he has eternality (always was and always will be). This belief is supported by the Bible and was further affirmed in AD 325 by the Council of Nicaea, which gave us the Nicene Creed; it has been adopted by practically all the denominations of Christendom as their own.

## Creation

God created the universe *ex nihilo*, out of nothing. He created the heavens and the earth and everything therein (John 1:3). God created not only a physical realm but also an unseen realm that includes angels and heaven (Nehemiah 9:6). God created Adam and Eve directly and mature; they did not evolve (1 Corinthians 11:8–9). God created all that is (Acts 17:25). Christians believe that creation reflects the Creator not as a self-portrait but as a reflection of his style, his loves, and his interests (Isaiah 43:7).

## Morals and Ethics

In Christianity, a life of good morals and high ethical practices is not only recommended but is essential. So how does one determine what is moral or ethical? Christians have the best possible example—Christ. Christians must strive to be Christlike in their lives. Will they ever meet that standard? No! But they must strive for it.

## Suffering and Evil

Non-Christians often point out that they are hard pressed to believe that an all-powerful, all-loving God would allow the rampant evil and suffering going on in the world. More often than not, Christians have fallen short in their response to this question.

Evil is not from God; evil is from humanity and Lucifer. It comes from humanity for its exercising its free will to take Lucifer up on his offer that people could become like God if they rejected him, and reject him they did.

Evil, therefore, is a direct result of humanity's rejection of God, the fall. Any moral choice has consequences. Since God cannot tolerate sin, he had to respond with punishment; otherwise, there would be no restraint on sinning. The consequences of sin are evil and suffering. God does not cause sin, but he allows its consequences to follow choices. God has provided a solution for us that we can partake of even in our fallen state.

## Salvation

Because of our fallen nature, our propensity to sin, we are unable to choose God and obey him through any of our own efforts or works. However, God wants us all to enjoy eternity with him in heaven (1 Timothy 2:3–4).

To this end, God came to earth as the incarnate Son, Jesus Christ, to reconcile humanity to himself. He thereby provided us with a choice we are capable of making even in our fallen state to accept by faith Jesus Christ as our Lord and Savior by believing in him.

By so doing, we can enjoy a restored fellowship with God, no longer blaming him for any evil or pain we might experience but thankful for his remedy of the problem of evil through his Son.

## Death and the Afterlife

It is appointed for man to die once and then the judgment.

Those who have believed in Christ will ultimately be judged to determine the level of rewards due. They will spend eternity in heaven in the company of the Lord and his saints. A saint is anyone who dies in Christ. Conversely, anyone who dies and has not accepted Christ will have a different fate.

> As the weeds are pulled up and burned in the fire, so it will be at the end of the age. The Son of Man will send out his angels, they will weed out of his kingdom everything that causes sin and all who do evil. They will throw them into the fiery furnace, where there will be weeping and gnashing of teeth. (Matthew 13:40–42)

## Christianity's Claims to Truth

Those who explain Christianity to nonbelievers use the Bible as their basis and proof of their beliefs. Thus, a skeptic need only prove biblical falsehood to disprove the validity of Christianity. Christianity stands or falls on the truthfulness of the Bible. A Christian accepts that the Bible is a book written by men inspired by God and that the Bible is in fact the Word of God.

Nonbelievers will invariably not accept the validity of the Bible based on the claims of the Bible or believers; they want secular proof. The Bible abounds with evidence and secular proof of its validity, authenticity, accuracy, and truthfulness. Some of the evidence answers the following key questions.

***Is the Bible we have today the same as the original?*** There are over 5,500 witnesses (ancient copies of the original manuscripts, partial manuscripts, and a fragment of the original New Testament writings) in existence today.

The Old Testament witnesses date back to 200 BC, while the New Testament witnesses date back to within a few decades of the original writings.

The rapid expansion of Christianity also meant a corresponding proliferation of copies of the original biblical manuscripts throughout the world.

When witnesses and their ensuing copies and various translations from all these different points of the globe are compared, their fidelity to each other proves beyond any reasonable doubt their accurate correspondence to the originals.

***Is there any evidence outside the Bible of its authenticity?*** Of the secular writers who provide nonbiblical corroboration to events surrounding the time of Jesus and immediately thereafter, Flavius Josephus (AD 37–100) is undoubtedly the best known. In his many writings, he wrote about the history of the Jews, the Jewish Messiah, the uprising of the Jews, and their complete defeat in AD 70.

Pliny the Younger (AD 60–112) was a Roman senator, a magistrate, a very successful Roman who held many other offices of import, and he was a prolific writer. He attested through references in his writings of the events around Christianity. Much of his correspondence has been preserved; some of it describes the continuing problems with Christians.

There are many other secular references to Jesus and his followers, and since a significant portion of these references are from the Roman perspective, they are not positive.

The fact is Jesus existed, the events in the Bible occurred, and the beginning of Christianity was witnessed from within the biblical perspective and outside the biblical perspective.

*Is the Bible historically accurate?* The archaeological record shows that all references to places, rulers, cultures, and nations (that have been tested) existed and occurred as depicted in the Bible. The record is so clear and convincing that we can say without equivocation that no archaeological discovery has ever been proven to controvert biblical scripture.

*Is there any scientific proof that corroborates biblical contents?* Before the world knew about harmful bacteria and about its potentially dreadful consequences, the Bible provided the Jews with very specific sanitation guidance, undoubtedly a contributing factor to their genealogical longevity. This was also a reason for the minimal impact the black plague had on the Jewish population during the Middle Ages.

Hundreds of years before Galileo and some two thousand years before Christopher Columbus, the book of Job told us the world was a sphere suspended in the heavens (does that sound like a flat earther to you?)

The Bible also plainly describes the earth's hydrological process (ocean water being drawn into the heavens, being deposited on the mountains and valleys, watering the plants and trees, and finding its way back whence it came) thousands of years before it was scientifically known. The list goes on and on. Yes, science has again and again proven the Bible's accuracy.

***And in the supernatural realm, what about biblical prophecies?*** The foretelling of the future is an area in which most people quickly exceed their comfort zone and is usually the point where they bail out of the conversation. Nonetheless, most religions practice prophecy, but all except Christianity have a dismal record.

Recorded in the Bible are hundreds of prophecies; all that have concerned events to the present have in fact taken place. Many of the prophecies that have taken place concerned Jesus and were made some 400 to 700 years before he was born. The prophecies specifically foretold the birth, life, ministry, death, and resurrection of Jesus.

Another prophecy many of us experienced or at least are knowledgeable of was the reuniting of the Jewish people in their own nation on a portion of the same land God bequeathed Abraham!

## Summary of Christianity

There is no doubt that if the Bible can be shown to be inaccurate and unreliable, Christianity, as a viable religion, would cease to exist (an answer to every atheist's prayer. But do atheists pray? If so, to whom?). To this end, there have been relentless and tenacious efforts to discredit the book that is the heart and soul of Christianity.

No other book ever has had anywhere near the scrutiny of this book, yet history has shown that it has withstood every onslaught thrown against it, and Christians know it will continue to do so.

# Chapter 14

# A Comparison of the Major Belief Systems

We have now briefly discussed each of the three major belief systems, and using the criteria established earlier, we will review their specific worldviews. I have summarized each of their worldviews on the specific criteria in the following tables. The following comments refer to the mentioned tables:

## God—Does He Exist or Not?

Atheists and naturalists state that God does not exist or that humanity itself is God. Pantheists say everything is God. Theists say there is only one God. The law of noncontradiction loudly proclaims that all these positions cannot be true, they may all be untrue, but since they are contradictory, no more than one can be true!

If only one can be true, how can we prove which one is true? In determining truth, we need to consider the disciplines we will be dealing with—religion and history, so we will have to resort to the law of probability.

*Point 1a.* Atheists' belief that there is no God is directly attributable to their denial of anything outside nature. However, nature, being restricted by its own laws, cannot account for the creation of matter or the start of life. Nature in fact denies that probability by its own first law of thermodynamics: you cannot create or destroy matter. Therefore, by the logical law of inference,

1.  Matter cannot be created.
2.  Humans are made of matter.
3.  Humans do not exist.

Continuing this inference, our life experiences prove that

1.  Humans do exist.
2.  Humans are made of matter.
3.  Nature cannot account for the creation of matter, therefore,
4.  Matter was created by something or someone outside of nature. If something is not natural, by definition, it must be supernatural. By this argument, we can conclude that matter was created supernaturally.

**Point 1b.** The pantheistic belief that everything is god and the theistic belief of one God can account for the supernatural creation of matter.

**Point 1c.** By the evidence presented so far, the first law of thermodynamics and the law of logical inference deny the atheistic viewpoint.

Table 1

|  | God | Creation | Morals/Ethics | Suffering and Evil | Salvation | Death and Afterlife | Claim to Truth |
|---|---|---|---|---|---|---|---|
| **Atheists** | There is no God. Man is the measure of all things | Universe always existed or big bang. People evolved. No souls. Higher than animals. | No standard of right and wrong, no moral absolute. | No right and wrong, hence sin and evil are relative. We are responsible for what we are or will be. | As material creatures, nothing to be saved from or to. End of people's lives is total realization of their personalities. | Death is the end of the line. No soul no afterlife. Life does not survive the death of the body. | True only if science says it's true. Truth is relative; no verifiable claims to truth. |
| **Pantheists** | There is a universal god. If it is not god, it is an illusion. You are god.<br><br>------<br><br>*PM: God is whoever you or your culture want it to be. | Created physical universe is an illusion. World is inseparable from god.<br><br>------<br><br>*PM: Relative, dependent on culture. | We should live moral lives, though morality is relative.<br><br>------<br><br>*PM: No moral absolute. Unable to judge evil or morality. | Being one with god, you exist beyond good and evil. Suffering is an illusion.<br><br>------<br><br>*PM: Determined by your culture. | To become one with god. Some through reincarnation<br><br>------<br><br>*PM: Whatever you want to believe. | Individual soul absorbed into soul of god; no personal identity.<br><br>------<br><br>*PM: Cultural beliefs determine reality of death and the afterlife. | All beliefs on faith only. No verifiable truth claims.<br><br>------<br><br>*PM: Rejection of all objective truth. |

**Postmodernism**

* 

103

Table 2

| | God | Creation | Morals/ Ethics | Suffering and Evil | Salvation | Death and Afterlife | Claim to Truth |
|---|---|---|---|---|---|---|---|
| **Monotheist Islamic** | Allah is only god. | Allah is creator and sustainer of the universe. | Muhammad exhorts Muslims to live good and moral lives. | It is good to suffer and even die for Allah. | Do good, fulfill five pillars, repent from sin, and remain faithful to Islam. | If good outweighs bad, by the grace of Allah, you might enter paradise. | Qur'an written years after one man (prophet) had revelation from God thru angel. |
| **Monotheist Judaist** | Only one God. No trinity. Jesus was prophet only. | God created the heavens and the earth. | Follow Ten Commandments and Mosaic Law. | Modern Judaism people not evil, misuse of nature generates evil. | Repent of your sins and follow God's laws and commandments. | Orthodox-resurrection of dead and eternal soul. Reformed- only spiritual life after death. | The Tanakh The Talmud The Oral Law. |
| **Monotheist Christian** | Only one God expressed in the trinity. | God created the universe (perhaps thru the big bang), the heavens, the earth, and everything therein. | Should live moral and ethical lives following Christ's example. | Result of the fall of humanity and the exercise of free will. | Belief in and acceptance of Christ through faith. | True believers to heaven. Nonbelievers to hell. | The Bible, historical, prophetic, evidential, and eyewitness proof. |

## Creation: The Universe, Humanity

Until the beginning of the twentieth century, atheists (including naturalists and secular humanists) generally claimed that the universe was eternal and had always existed. The prevalent theory now is in the big bang theory. Pantheists claim that the universe is one with god, and if it is not one with god, it is an illusion, while postmodernists believe that whatever your culture believes is the way it is (i.e., the truth). Theists believe that God (Allah for Muslims) created the universe; most theological scholars do not exclude the big bang theory from the creation process.

Obviously, the law of noncontradiction states that the above cannot all be true! But this time, classical science joins the mix. If something has existed forever, it means it is very, very old. The first law of thermodynamics states that energy/matter in the universe is constant. The second law states that in our closed universe, the ever-increasing rate of entropy (decay) makes the usefulness of energy transfer less and less viable as time goes on to the point that can be called the death of the universe.

Since the universe is obviously not dead, science flatly states that the universe cannot have existed forever. For big bang adherents, science still says you cannot create matter, so where did it come from? I think I recollect that both atheists and naturalists state that if science says it is so, then it has to be.

Atheists (secular humanists and naturalists included) believe that humanity evolved. The beginning of the evolutionary process is not so clear, though. Richard Dawkins, the self-proclaimed spokesman for atheism, says that the evolutionary process probably originated with some kind of primordial soup. The usual scenario has the crashing of ocean waves onto shore, leaving water collected in rock crevices. Exposure to the elements turned this water into a soupy sludge. On a dark, turbulent, stormy night, lightning struck the rock, and the soupy mixture transformed into a living organism!

Dawkins was reminded of the extensive scientific experimentation in the 1950s that tried to recreate this scenario. They proved that the extreme heat that would have been generated by lightning produced only highly noxious chemicals not conducive to the generation of life but to the eradication of any potential organic substance. Mr. Dawkins then stated that perhaps aliens had brought life (anything except God!). End of conversation.

Pantheists are more ambivalent about the start of humanity, leaving it up to the various cultures to explain it. Theists share the belief of a creator and a creation. Man was created by God. Most theists agree with the general biblical account of the Old Testament but not so much on its timing or duration.

So again, we are presented with a highly divergent set of beliefs. Science does not prove but tends to disprove the primordial soup theory. And we haven't even brought up the DNA conundrum for evolutionists—yet. Science cannot prove or disprove any occurrence or event beyond the natural, and I think we can all agree God's creation of the universe, humanity, and all else that exists is beyond the natural. Again, to establish truth, we will have to resort to the law of probability, but this time, we will be able to draw on scientific evidence—the archaeological record.

***Point 2a.*** The atheistic original belief that the universe had always existed was not supported by the first and second laws of thermodynamics. The first law states that matter in the universe is constant. The second law states that in essence, through the concept of entropy (accelerating decay), the universe is dying. Logical inference then shows that since the universe is decaying, since matter in the universe cannot be replenished, and since the universe is not dead, it must therefore be concluded that the universe had a beginning (it has not existed forever). Since it had a beginning, natural laws require that it must have been a supernatural beginning. The atheists who now believe in the big bang theory still have the problem of creation of matter. Where did it come from?

***Point 2b.*** The evolution of humanity is replete with scientific evidence, but not for it— against it! Other than an almost insatiable desire on some people's part to find scientific evidence for it, it has little support. Nonetheless, it appears that most of humanity demands that we find something, anything, to prove that humans were not created!

Our schools, especially our universities, are blind proponents of this theory. The professors have their books, glossy pictures, and charts, most of which are grossly exaggerated or downright false. For example, take the "geological column," which is presented as archaeological proof of the evolution of life by its categorization of different stages of evolution in a "core" with horizontal lines representing eons of time. This core is supposed to represent a core drilling of the earth from the surface to an undetermined depth with representations of the evolution of life through the different archaeological periods. Most natural history museums will have this column conspicuously presented. This is all totally subjective and represents nothing more than what they hope to find but nonetheless presented by academia as fact.

The "tree of evolution" is much like the geological column but normally shows only interesting colorful drawings of the evolution of man. Again, it is totally subjective, almost completely without proof, and yet normally presented as proof of evolution!

The "archaeological record" contains several hundred years of intense searching for a "missing" link that would prove evolution between different species, but not one shred of true evidence has been found. I say "true" because there have been several dramatic finds that purported to show definitive proof of this interspecies evolution that turned out to be concocted.

The highly trumpeted Piltdown Man comes to mind. In 1911 and 1912 "fossils" were found in England and were hailed as the earliest Englishman and believed to be the missing link. The parts of a skull (from which innumerable sketches and glossy, full-body drawings of our "ancestor" were made) turned out to be from a modern ape that had been treated with chemicals to make them look old; this was reported in the New York times on November 21, 1953. No doubt some of these glossies are still sitting around in our ivy-clad halls of academia and being passed off as proof of evolution. Java Man was finally accepted as the remains of a giant gibbon, a small ape. The large, stooped-over brute we came to know as Neanderthal Man turned out to be parts of a large, severely arthritic human skeleton. It goes without saying that the corrections to these findings were not nearly as widely broadcast as the original, highly acclaimed releases.

Besides the interspecies evolutionary problem, a real setback for evolutionists came with the discovery of what is known as the Cambrian Explosion. This finding showed that huge numbers of different species were found in full stages of development all at one time within a relatively short timeframe; they showed no signs of evolving. Charles Darwin did acknowledge that this finding did in fact present a significant problem for his theory of evolution. But he, along with his followers, felt confident that in time, proof of his theory would be discovered in the fossil record. All findings to date have posed additional problems for his theory.

***The Eye, DNA, and Irreducible Complexity.*** The theory of irreducible complexity states that certain key elements of life (or things) cannot be reduced and have any function that resembles the end item. The human eye is an item that could not have evolved into anything like the eye we have now. Our eye is connected to our brain with an estimated 125,000,000 nerve endings in a very specific sequence! Do we really believe that random chance could have created the eye? The statistical probability of this happening is so huge that it is nonexistent.

Another, perhaps more-cogent, example of irreducible complexity is the very simple mousetrap. Its basic components are a piece of wood, a coiled spring, a high-tensile wire, and food holder/wire release. On their own, they are not a mousetrap. We can sit there forever watching to see if the piece of wood will miraculously grow the other components. Better yet, you sit there and watch it; I'm not going to. Only when you carefully assemble the various components in their specific places will you have a mousetrap. Yes, this also basically describes intelligent design.

The discovery of DNA should have had even the most ardent evolutionist throw in the proverbial towel! But the acceptance of a creator was unthinkable! So, with the knowledge that even the one-cell amoeba has enough coded information stored in its DNA to fill up several volumes of the *Britannica Encyclopedia*, evolutionists still cling to their theory.

Furthermore, this DNA has a key code that directs the growth process (in the case of humans) determining the sex, hair color, etc., of the baby. This code can be provided only by its parents. You have to be an ardent evolutionist to be capable of believing that a wet rock struck by lightning provided your key code!

So this is probably the kind of thinking my elementary schoolteacher was using when she told the class that wild monkeys banging on typewriters (*way* before iPads) if given enough time could produce a complete Shakespearean play! At age eleven, I didn't believe it, and I still don't any more than I believe a tornado going through an automobile junkyard could produce a Boeing 747.

An additional clarifying point is necessary regarding interspecies evolution. Evolutionists often claim that there is already ample evidence of interspecies evolution. They will then point to the many breeds of dogs—some small, some hairy, etc.—the cross breeding of farm animals, and so on. But this is possible only within a species. You can't breed a cat with a bird and get a cat that flies!

Saying that each different breed of dog is its own specific specie is tantamount to altering the meaning of words to support a fallacious argument. Furthermore, these changes in species are not a natural phenomenon; they are possible only through much thought, study, and research. Did I just define intelligent design again?

There is no doubt that microevolution (minor changes *within* a species) is a reality. To a limited degree, life has the ability to adapt to its surroundings; this is called survival. This ability is further evidence of intelligent design.

So has evolution been totally disproven? No. Statistically, it is possible, though that possibility is infinitesimally small. As far as probability, the statistical evidence is so overwhelmingly against it that it is out of the realm of probability. Additionally, scientific studies attempting to recreate the evolutionary theory of the start of life have provided data that only disproves the theory. Therefore, using the laws of probability, a reasonable person would conclude that the evolutionary theory of the start of life and the possibility of interspecies evolution is not possible.

We should not conclude this discussion on evolution without pointing out some of the major consequences of the evolutionary theory. Evolution depends on "survival of the fittest" to "improve" human genetics. The eugenics movement (improvement of the human race) can be directly traced to this philosophy in no small part because of Darwin's belief that inferior races would in the future be destroyed by superior races.

Margaret Sanger, founder of Planned Parenthood, in *Woman and the New Race*, stated, "[We should] apply a stern and rigid policy of sterilization and segregation to that grade of population whose progeny is tainted, or whose inheritance is such that objectionable traits may be transmitted to offspring." In the *Birth Control Review* dated April 1932, she wrote, "Birth control must lead ultimately to a cleaner race."

Other ardent adherents to the eugenics philosophy of eliminating tainted, thus inferior, humans include such notables as Joseph Stalin, believed to have eliminated over 115 million people, and Adolph Hitler, who eliminated over 12 million.

In 1966, Planned Parenthood instituted its highest annual award, the Margaret Sanger Award.

The pantheistic beliefs on how the universe or the inhabitants of the world came to be cannot be proven or disproven because of their ambivalence. Because truth is relative, we cannot criticize anyone's beliefs; any culture can believe as it wishes.

Scientifically, the logical law of noncontradiction proves that all these differing beliefs cannot be true; only one may be true. And, referring to the logical law of inference we see that

1.  the theistic belief that the universe and everything therein was created by a supreme being;
2.  the scientific community's inability to show that natural causes could have created the universe from nothing, their own laws in fact showing that natural causes could not have created the universe; and
3.  the scientific community's inability to create life from lifeless matter, while their own tests confirm that in nature, you cannot create life from lifeless matter

lead us to conclude that the universe and the life therein was created outside of nature (i.e., supernaturally, by God).

## Morals and Ethics—Absolute or Relative?

Atheists and pantheists do not have a clear standard of what constitutes good and acceptable morals and ethics. Atheists generally believe that morals and ethics are derived from human experience, needs, and interests, so there are no absolute morals and ethics, only what comes naturally.

They also believe that past religious beliefs have been unnaturally restrictive on natural, human proclivities. If it does not harm anyone, feel free to do it! Postmodernists hang on to no moral absolute or standard other than what any one culture adopts. Not only must we not judge right and wrong for others, since morals and ethics are relative, we *can't* judge!

Theists are much more resolute in their beliefs. Morals and ethics are established by the Creator. They are absolute—not staying in the parameters established by these absolutes will bear consequences.

Can we envision a world with no absolute moral standards? If there are no moral standards, on what should we base our laws? Wait a second now. We all know we can't legislate morality, right? Let's think about it for a second. If we study our laws, we will see that generally they tend to eliminate or at least temper immoral acts.

Let's look at a moral standard we can all recognize, the Ten Commandments; thou shalt not steal—we have laws against stealing; thou shalt not bear false witness—we have laws against perjury; thou shalt not commit murder—we have laws against manslaughter, wrongful death, and homicide. No doubt we can go on and on, but I trust the point is made. Are we successful at legislating morality? That's a whole other story.

Without moral standards, we could not judge the Hitlers, the Stalins, the Idi Amins, or the Saddam Husseins of the world. Without moral standards, we could certainly envision a constant deterioration into anarchy.

**Point 3a.** Atheists, naturalists, modernists, pantheists, et al. are pretty much in accord on their belief of relativism; some are more ardent than others, but the general belief is there. If morals and ethics are relative, the question arises, relative to what? The obvious answer is relative to what you think is right. So if you think it's moral, it's moral; if you think it's ethical, it's ethical.

Having established that, let's do a little internal soul searching. (Sorry, I misspoke. You true atheists don't have souls.) Are you happy with your moral and ethical standards? Do you feel confident that your standards will serve you, your family, and your progeny well throughout your lives? Unless you're honest, your answers will be meaningless.

To attempt to try to prove or disprove the validity of the relativism belief, we have to look beyond laws and look to the particular worldviews that give rise to the relativism concept. To help each one of us ascertain the validity of relativism to us personally, we have to truthfully answer the following questions.

1. Does my worldview endorse a lifestyle that is in my family's and my best interests?
2. Do the results of the decisions I make adhering to this worldview provide emotional and spiritual satisfaction to my family and me?
3. Do the results of these decisions support and fulfill my instinctive needs, which include protecting, providing, nourishing, and satisfying the needs of my family?

If you can answer all the above questions in the affirmative, chances are excellent that you are on solid footing with your worldview. If you honestly answered all the questions in the affirmative, you *cannot* believe in relativism. The reason is simple: if there is no moral absolute and you accept everybody's right to establish his or her own morals and ethics without recourse, you can imagine the outcome. In a relatively short period, pornography, theft, assault, murder, debauchery, and all actions we now call crimes would be rampant. It's frightening to realize just how close we are to what I have just described.

A seemingly reasonable person would say, "We'll never let it get that far!" I say to them, "You don't believe in relativism, you actually believe you should be given the right to set your own morals and ethics, but everybody else will need to adhere to your standards!"

As difficult as it might be for you to accept, relativism does not work. To have a valid, functioning society, some authority has to set a moral standard.

***Point 3b.*** Of the three belief systems we have been discussing, only theists believe in an absolute moral standard. For those of you who may still have a hard time accepting set standards in morals and ethics, I encourage you to read the story of Liberal, Missouri. George H. Walser, a lawyer and atheist, purchased land in 1880 to establish a completely secular town. Unencumbered by "judgmental Christians," he wanted only "free thinkers." The founder allowed no priests, preachers, churches, saloons, God, Jesus, hell, or the devil.

Within five years, drunkenness was common, promiscuous sex was rampant, townsfolk constantly swore, the only hotel became a brothel, children rebelled against their parents and swore habitually, and the townspeople even practiced feticide! What is feticide? That practice now goes by the more genteel and less offensive name of pro-choice. It's an interesting read. Liberal, Missouri still exists; the population is now about 800, and seven churches are within its boundary. Its founder? Well, he became a Christian, and in 1909, he wrote a book, *The Life and Teachings of Jesus.*

So yes, we do have empirical evidence of what happens when you do away with moral and ethical standards.

## Suffering and Evil—Real or Illusions?

Naturalists tend to see suffering as part of the evolutionary process of survival of the fittest. Pantheists rationalize that since the universal God is everything spiritual and has no feelings, suffering is an illusion. God is not a moral being, so once you become one with God, you move beyond good and evil. Theists all believe there is suffering and evil. There are disparities in cause and effect of suffering and evil, at least between the followers of the Qur'an and the Bible. Nonetheless, theists don't doubt the existence of suffering and evil.

**Point 4a.** The human experience has shown beyond any doubt (reasonable or otherwise) that there is pain and suffering and that there is evil. To claim that suffering is an illusion or does not exist exceeds credulity. Do Christian Scientists go to the hospital when they break an arm or a leg? Or do they disregard the excruciating pain as an illusion? With the growing number of pantheists and postmodernists, perhaps our national health care costs really will go down.

The logical law known as self-evident propositions and Descartes's first principle law prove that pain and suffering exist because you can feel it and it hurts!

**Point 4b.** Does evil exist? How do we know it exists? If there were nothing but evil, perhaps we would not be aware that evil existed. However, there is good, and because there is good, we know evil exists. Furthermore, we are able to measure and judge evil by the standard known as good.

## Salvation: Eternal Life?

Atheists, naturalists, and secular humanists see nothing beyond this life. We are matter without any soul or spiritual being. We die and it's over. Pantheists, on the other hand, see salvation as becoming one with the universal God. Theists believe in salvation. How one attains salvation, though, differs greatly.

**Point 5a.** The concept of salvation is widely misunderstood. To those who believe in an afterlife, salvation usually means understanding what it takes to ensure that the afterlife will be a pleasant experience rather than an unpleasant one or worse, a painful one. It is important to know how to get there, but it is much more important to know what you have to do to get there. Atheists do not believe in an afterlife, so they are not in this discussion. Their not being a part of the discussion or their unbelief does not imply that there is no afterlife for the atheist, everybody will have an afterlife!

**Point 5b.** Pantheists and theists each believe there is something after this life but differ greatly in how to get to the right place.

1. For pantheists, the point is to live a moral life and get close to the universal god.
2. Islamists strive to live a moral life, do the five pillars, travel to Mecca, and if Allah thinks they've done enough, they will be saved.
3. Jews achieve paradise by obeying the Ten Commandments, Mosaic Law, the Talmud, and the Oral Law.
4. Christians get to heaven by believing in Jesus. This belief will lead them to loving God with all their heart, soul, and mind and to loving their neighbors as themselves.

**Point 5c.** The law of noncontradiction again proclaims that all may be wrong but only one can be right.

## Death and the Afterlife—Is Death the End?

Death is inescapable, and atheists, naturalists, and secular humanists don't believe in an afterlife. If there is no afterlife, if what we do in this life is all there is, what's it all about? What's the point? Is this the end of our journey? What kind of a cruel joke is this? We're born, we struggle in growing up, school, more school, work, buy things, work, pay bills, work, have kids, work, get old, and then die! Is that all there is to life?

Pantheists also believe that death is inevitable, but they believe in an afterlife that consists of an absorption of the individual soul into the universal God, thus completely losing their identities, consciousness, and the ability to process thought; they cease to exist.

Muslims, Jews, and Christians share a belief in the certainty of death and an afterlife. For Christians, death is a certainty for all unless they are alive when Jesus returns for the second time.

**Point 6a.** The final destinations for those who made the proper choice(s) include the following.

1. Pantheists: Believing that God is everything and everywhere, they will simply be absorbed into the universal god for all eternity. No family reunion, just a oneness with the universal god.
2. Muslims: Having fulfilled the requirements delineated by Muhammad, those deemed faithful, by the grace of Allah, will enter paradise, a place of fruit, rivers, cushions and carpets, and maidens pure and holy.
3. Jews: Orthodox Jews believe in a bodily resurrection followed by an eternity with God. Reformed Jews do not believe in the resurrection of the body but believe in the eternality of the soul, which will spend eternity with God.
4. Christians: Having believed in Jesus, upon their death, their souls will immediately go to heaven. When Christ returns, they will be bodily resurrected and will spend eternity with all believers and with God the Father, Son, and Holy Spirit.

**Point 6b.** Pantheists and postmodernists are okay with whatever you want to believe; Muslims believe that if you are not a Muslim, you will go to hell; Jews do not believe that Jesus is God; and Christians believe that believing in Jesus is the only way to salvation from eternal damnation.

Being tolerant of everyone's views and beliefs does not make everyone's views true (right). We know rather emphatically by now that when two or more views contradict each other in the same time and in the same essence, only one can be true; they can all be wrong, but only one can be true.

## The Analysis

So based on the information, presented, which of the above beliefs has the highest probability of being right and/or true?

***Fact 1.*** Scientific research, archaeology, statistical analysis, the law of probability, and natural law combine to show that the two main underpinnings of atheism (naturalism, secular humanism, et al.), which are that the universe has existed forever or that it was created from nothing through the big bang theory, and how life started and the evolution of man, are not possible and could not have occurred naturally. Therefore, since the universe, life, and humanity exist, if they did not occur naturally, they must have and did occur supernaturally. Without these two underpinnings and the fact that atheists unabashedly exclude any belief in the supernatural, we must conclude that the atheistic belief is false.

***Fact 2.*** Taken to the extreme, the ambivalence of pantheism and postmodernism, their tendency to accept almost anything as true, their worldview on total tolerance, their rejection of absolute moral or ethical standards, their acceptance of and continuing efforts to impose political correctness on our society, and their wholehearted acceptance of relativism would not only be detrimental to our society but could almost certainly lead to the end of our society as we know it and as our forefathers established and envisioned it.

On the surface, pantheism and postmodernism sound very enlightening, very intellectual, and very easy to accept, and millions upon millions have. Notwithstanding the emotive draw of pantheism and postmodernism, the worldview that leads to their acceptance does not fulfill the requirements necessary to categorize it as good for us, our families, and our society. A society ensconced in lawlessness, debauchery, debasement of the family, deceit, immorality, and godlessness is certainly not conducive to a society in which we would like to raise our families and live our lives. For these reasons, this belief system must be categorized as unacceptable.

***Fact 3.*** Islam is a religion that almost exclusively depends on the validity of the Qur'an for its own validity. Muhammad was the sole author of the Qur'an; its contents, he claims, were revealed over several years to him exclusively in a cave by the angel Gabriel—no bystanders, no witnesses. These revelations were written down by the fourth leader of the Muslims many years after Muhammad died.

The religion is spread by word and by sword—by force. In the Qur'an, women are inferior to men, converts can be converted by force, deceit against non-Muslims is acceptable, and Muslims can leave Islam only under the penalty of death.

***Fact 4.*** Judaism is the oldest established religion. The Tanakh, the Hebrew Bible, which is the same as the Christian Old Testament, is its holy scripture. It was written over an eleven-hundred-year period by some thirty-two authors. An abundance of secular and biblical witnesses attest to its historicity, its authorship, and its overall validity, which is supplemented by archaeological proof.

The Tanakh teaches Jews how to live holy lives, how to worship God, and how to raise their families. Though they will accept non-Jews into their religion (after they fulfill all of the requirements), they do not go out of their way to seek converts; they pretty much keep it in the family. As mentioned elsewhere in this discussion, their durability and tenacity is exceeded only by their impact on the world financially and politically and to a significant degree militarily.

***Fact 5.*** Biblically, Christianity is a continuation of the Jewish Tanakh. The Christian Bible contains the same Old Testament (OT) with a continuation of the scriptures in the New Testament (NT). Almost all of the eight NT authors make references to OT personalities and scriptures. The God in the OT is the same God in the NT. The Messiah (God the Son) is present in the OT (to a large degree through prophesy) and is exceedingly prominent in the NT. We have mentioned that the Tanakh (OT) is abundantly supported by secular and biblical proof, and the NT secular proof dwarfs the OT proof in validity and authenticity.

Though the whole Bible sets the mold and standards for Christianity, the NT sharpens and defines the Christian. The NT provides guidance for the Christian, explains how to become a Christian, how to establish and grow a relationship with God, and how to bring new converts to Christianity. There is no denying that the OT records some acts that are undoubtedly cruel, but most are descriptive and not directive in nature. The few that are recorded as divinely directive were to remove cultures that had completely rejected God and had sunk to a level of sin, lawlessness, and debauchery from which there was no return. Throughout the NT, the underlying theme is respect, gentleness, and above all, love.

## Conclusion of the Analysis

This discussion has shown that atheism is rejected by its own rules. Pantheism and postmodernism have as their claims to truth that truth is relative or nonexistent and that you should believe as they do … because you should. They maintain that since truth is nonexistent, since morals and ethics are relative, and since logic doesn't apply because you have to go beyond logic to understand, you cannot use those standards to measure their belief systems. Furthermore, it feels good because it is nonthreatening to their desires, tolerant of everybody's choices, and completely nonjudgmental. A logical and reasonable mind would conclude that complete acceptance of their beliefs will lead our society and culture into areas we do not want to go. Hence, the logical mind must reject the basis for this belief system and ultimately the belief system itself.

Islam, with its official and often direct dependence on brutality to achieve its objectives, its subjugation of nearly half its adherents (women), and its professed intent to dominate the world with its laws, has to be treated as a direct threat to our society, culture, and nation. Furthermore, from a secular perspective, when we look at the evidence supporting the probability of the authenticity of its source of belief, it's subjective at best.

Judaism is not seeking to grow by means of conversions. Jews are busy coalescing their Jewish brethren from the many nations to which they were dispersed and meeting and rebuking their neighbors' constant threats to their very survival. Nevertheless, in accordance with the NT, they still have a major role to play as we approach the end-time.

Christianity uses secular tools and historical documentation to point out the historicity of many of the people and events described in the Bible; they existed and occurred as depicted. They point to the archaeological evidence of the existence of the places described in the Bible and the secular documentation showing that Jesus existed at the time and place described in the Bible. Christians also believe that the people who followed Jesus considered him to be the Messiah referred to in the OT, that he was crucified and buried, and that his followers attested that on the third day he resurrected. Although many of the people who witnessed these events were still alive after the writings, none refuted their accuracy. Therefore, using the logical law of inference, having proven that the above premises are true, we must accept that the Bible is true.

Having provided secular, thus objective, evidence that much of the Bible is true, and although people have tried for countless years to find evidence to disprove any portion of the testable Bible, by the laws of probability, the evidence brings the probability of validity to a level of certainty that approaches the absolute and leads us to the only possible conclusion—all of the Bible is true. All of this from external, secular evidence.

And finally the law of noncontradiction. Atheists say there is no God. Pantheists say everything is God, postmodernists say God is whatever, Muslims say Allah is the only God, Judaism says that the

God of the OT is the only God, and Christians state that God is the only God and that he is the God of the OT and the NT and that God consists of God the Father, Son, and Holy Spirit.

Since all these beliefs contradict each other and knowing that all can be false but only one if any can be true, based on the evidence, we must conclude that the Judeo/Christian God of the OT and NT is the one true God, that there is a heaven and a hell, and that we will go to one or the other. There is no other choice.

Truth is reality. For us to accept reality, the will must cooperate with the mind!

## Review of Part 3

1. What are the three major belief systems?
2. Define atheism.
3. Postmodernism has seen explosive growth in the past fifty years. Give three reasons why you think it is so alluring to the general population.
4. In number of adherents, which are the two largest theistic religions?
5. What are the two largest Islamic sects?
6. Name three of the five pillars of Islam.
7. The Jewish temple has been destroyed twice. When was the last time? Has it been rebuilt?
8. What emperor made Christianity the official religion of Rome? What year?
9. Define Christianity.
10. What is the current secular belief concerning the creation of the universe?
11. Regarding Darwin's theory of evolution, describe what is meant by the "missing link."
12. Can you have morals without a standard? Explain.

# Part 4:

## Christianity

## Overview of Part 4

You have seen how supremely solid the foundation of Christianity is especially when compared with all the other religions. The indisputable proof, the unimpeachable validity, and the preponderance of verifiable truths attest to the character, perfection, and foresight of its Founder and namesake. If you have let your will cooperate with your mind, you could arrive at no other conclusion. Reality is truth.

## Christian

This term, meant to be derogatory, was first used in Antioch just a few years after the resurrection and ascension of Christ. The word *Christ* came from the Hebrew word for Messiah, which meant "the anointed one." As mentioned earlier before they were known as Christians they were simply called people of "the Way," since they knew the way to eternal life.

The Old Testament's first prophecy of the coming Messiah is in Genesis 3:15, when God rebuked Satan for deceiving Eve: "I will put enmity between you and the woman, and between your offspring and hers, he [the Messiah] will crush your head."

Jesus was born in Bethlehem about 3 BC of Jewish parents. At that time, Israel had been under Roman rule for many years. Shortly after his birth, to survive an attempt by King Herod on the child's life, his family fled to Egypt. After King Herod's death, they moved back to Judea and settled in Nazareth, where he picked up his father's carpentry trade.

Even at age twelve, Jesus' knowledge of scripture was evidenced when, on one of his family's trips to Jerusalem to celebrate Passover, he was separated from his family. After much searching, his family found him in the temple fully discussing scripture with the elders and leaders of the temple. The record shows the leaders were astonished at his knowledge of the scriptures.

His next appearance occurred when John the Baptist baptized him in the Jordan when he was thirty. The Bible tells us that after his baptism he went into the desert wilderness and fasted and prayed for forty days. Toward the end of the forty days, while he was weak and famished from his fasting, Satan tempted and taunted him. Overcoming each temptation with quotes from scripture, Satan left him. The angels then attended to his needs. Jesus then started his ministry.

Early in his ministry, and while walking along the Sea of Galilee, he saw two fishermen, Cephas [whom he would rename Peter] and his brother Andrew, they unhesitatingly responded to his simple command "follow me". As they continued along the banks of the sea they came across two other fishermen, John and his brother James, they also quickly responded to his "follow me" command. And so it went as Jesus continued his ministry throughout Galilee. When he saw a man he wanted in his ministry he would simply command him to "follow me". Not one of the twelve Apostles ever hesitated

Jesus preached a gospel of love, service, and humility while performing countless healings and other miracles. During the three years of his ministry, huge crowds gathered to hear him. This also drew the attention of the Jewish religious leaders who would become very concerned about his popularity and the new religion he was spreading.

These leaders rejected the possibility that Jesus could have been the long-awaited Messiah because his message was all wrong and he was obviously not the warrior/king they anticipated whom they believed would free them from the yoke of Roman rule. And certainly Jesus and his common and uneducated followers were certainly not the ones that would reestablish the kingdom of Israel. His message of love, service, and humility ran contrary to their expectations!

Jesus often chastised the religious leaders for being more interested in their own power and traditions then in worshipping God. Infuriated, the religious leaders began looking for a way to have him silenced. When Jesus claimed he was the son of God, the Sanhedrin (religious leaders) put him on trial for blasphemy, convicted him, and turned him over to Pontius Pilate on a charge of sedition. Reluctantly, and making a public statement of his objection by washing his hands in view of the crowd, Pilate commanded that Jesus be flogged and crucified.

Jesus was crucified, buried, and on the third day resurrected. He appeared to his apostles (eleven since Judas Iscariot had betrayed Jesus and committed suicide), other disciples, some of the women who had supported him, and five hundred other followers. He then ascended into heaven.

Christianity grew rapidly. Nonetheless, the second and third centuries saw an astounding escalation of persecutions against Christians resulting in a great number of executions.

In the fourth century, with Emperor Constantine's conversion to Christianity, persecutions essentially ceased. This led to even more-rapid growth. The first major tension in the church came between the Eastern (which became known as the Greek Orthodox Church) and Western (later known as the Roman Catholic Church) churches with differences of opinion on certain worship procedures. There have been some recent attempts at reconciliation.

Even with this major split Christianity continued its growth. In time several groups of people began to believe the church was drifting away from the basic Christian doctrine established by its founder, Jesus. This concept came to a head when in the sixteenth century a German monk, Martin Luther, thought the church had drifted too far away from biblical guidance and doctrine and sought to bring the church back to basic biblical worship. This confrontation gave rise to the Reformation which in turn led to the third major Christian group, the Protestants. Notwithstanding this splintering, Christianity has grown to become the largest religion in the world.

# Chapter 15

# The Bible—Myth, Fiction, or Truth?

Christianity stands or falls on the validity of the Bible. If the Bible can be shown to be based on myth, half-truths, or fantasy, Christianity as we know it would cease to exist. So let's take a look at this book from antiquity that claims to be a story of humanity not only from the start but all the way to the end of the human race, a book on how to live a good and fruitful life, a book on how to live in eternity with the Creator.

Who were the authors? When did they write the books included in the Bible? And to whom did they write their stories? We will look at the authors of the Bible books included in the canon. (At the Council of Trent in 1546, the Roman Catholic Church added several books to the Bible, but we will discuss these later). There are sixty-six books in the original canon of the Bible, thirty-nine in the Old Testament, and twenty-seven in the New Testament.

## The Authors

The thirty-nine books of the Old Testament were written by kings (King David, King Solomon), prophets (Moses, Isaiah, Ezekiel, Jeremiah, Micah, and others), and judges (Judges were the leaders of the Jewish nation before they had kings).

The twenty-seven books of the New Testament were written by apostles (Matthew, John, Peter, and Paul), close associates of apostles (Mark, who was mentored by the apostle Peter, and Luke, who was the apostle Paul's personal physician and aide), and two of Jesus' four brothers, James and Jude.

The first four books (known as the gospel) of the New Testament are the most bibliographic, giving us the story of Jesus. The word *gospel* means "good news."

The apostle Matthew wrote the first of the four gospel books that bear his name. He wrote his book to a Jewish audience; it is considered an excellent transition from the Old Testament to the New Testament. Although his book is the first in the New Testament, scholars believe that it was written in the 80s.

The second gospel was written by Mark, who wrote for a Roman audience. Scholars believe his was the first gospel book written in the 70s, some thirty-seven years after the ascension of Christ. The book is fast paced and cryptic.

The third gospel was written by Luke, generally accepted as a renowned academic and historian, with the Gentiles (non-Jewish people) as his audience. His book is the longest of the Gospels and is very specific in terms of names of people and places. Luke's gospel was written in the 80s. He also wrote the book of Acts, which some scholars believe is a continuation of his original book, which carries his name. Throughout the ages, his books have been used as references and guides for Israeli historical information.

The apostle John wrote the fourth gospel along with four other New Testament books: 1 John, 2 John, 3 John, and the book of Revelation. John's gospel differs from the other three gospels in that it was written years after the other three (in the 90s) and has a more-spiritual and broader perspective possibly because John was one of the three apostles (the other two were John's brother James and Peter) who had the closest relationship with Jesus.

John and his brother James were apparently a handful because Jesus often referred to them as "Sons of Thunder." This and other similar references indicate that Jesus had a sense of humor.

### Other New Testament Authors

In the book of Acts (also known by its longer title, Acts of the Apostles), Luke carried the story forward from the resurrection of Jesus and his appearances and contacts with his disciples and other followers who would play a vital role in the growth and spread of Christianity. He tells us about the first church leaders, their problems and continuing persecutions and how they overcame them, and the establishment of the first churches.

The apostle Paul was the most prolific writer of the New Testament authors; he is credited with writing fourteen of the twenty-seven New Testament books. There are, however, some scholars who doubt he was the author of the book of Hebrews; some scholars believe Barnabas could be the author. Jesus' brothers James and Jude each wrote one book that bears each one's name. The apostle Peter wrote 1 and 2 Peter.

### Credibility of the Authors

As we look at the credentials of the authors, we can see that these writers were certainly involved and would have had direct or personal knowledge of the material they wrote about, with the possible exception of Moses and the first of his five Old Testament books, Genesis. This, however, does not make Genesis any less credible than the other biblical books since critical knowledge was provided to him in several ways, some of which were through theophanies, that is, appearances by God in a form visible to man but not necessarily material.

Although the Bible was written by forty authors over a period of approximately fourteen hundred years, with its context, continuity, and syntax, it reads as if its sixty-six books were authored (inspired) by one person, and Christians believe it was.

## From Antiquity

The Bible comprises some of the oldest books known to man. Other books that reach out to us from antiquity include Homer's Iliad (written around 750 BC) and his Odyssey (believed to have been written around 720 BC) and the writings of Confucius (551 BC to 479 BC). The authorship of the first five books of the Bible, as previously stated, was attributed to Moses. These books were written around 1250–1225 BC, some five hundred years earlier than the next oldest recorded book, Homer's Iliad.

Skeptics have stated that some of the beginnings of the Bible bear an uncanny resemblance to Greek mythology presumably because the Iliad deals with the story of the ending of the Trojan War and the interaction with the Greek gods and humanity during and after this war. An objective look at the timeline shows that if anything, the opposite is closer to the truth.

## Did Moses Write the Law Books?

Critics have stated that Moses could not have written any of the books attributed to him because there was no alphabet or any means by which to write during his lifetime. The archaeological record does not support this criticism. The earliest examples of hieroglyphic inscriptions on clay tablets take us back to Egypt and Mesopotamia around 3000 BC. Tombs, monuments, and temples attest to stories being told in rather complex hieroglyphs even earlier by many hundreds of years.

Although the person or persons who came up with the first alphabet are unknown, archaeologists believe the first alphabet came from the Syria/Palestine area around 1750 BC. Alphabetic script has been found on inscriptions on rock tablets not far from Mount Sinai and dating to 1500 BC. On Mount Sinai, Moses received the Ten Commandments written on stone tablets by God's own finger approximately 300 years later.

## The Writing Material

Paper as we know it didn't exist during this period, so ancient writers used available material. One of the earliest known writing materials was, as stated above, stone. King Hammurabi of Babylon erected a stone monument with all his laws so his subjects would know and obey them. The monument is estimated to have been erected around 1750 BC. One of the earliest Hebrew inscriptions on stone is the Gezer Calendar, from around 925 BC, during the reign of King Solomon.

Clay was even a more popular ancient writing material. Tablets were made from clay, written on, then baked and stored. Several hundred clay tablets dating to 1350 BC were discovered in Egypt; they were correspondence between Egyptian rulers and surrounding dignitaries.

Besides stone and clay, the ancients inscribed their words on wood planks and metal, especially for official inscriptions. Roman soldiers, upon discharge, were given small, bronze tablets showing their service and granting them citizenship and other special privileges.

A more common and less costly writing material was *ostraca*. This material consisted of potsherds (broken pottery). The next material became the material of choice for writers; papyrus was inexpensive, light, easy to write on, and easy to carry. *Biblion* was the Greek word for a roll of papyrus. *Biblia* was the term for the plural papyrus rolls, and from this word we get *Bible.*

More-expensive rivals of papyrus were leather and parchment. Leather was of course more durable. As the availability of papyrus dwindled, leather became the material of choice. From the fourth century AD on, we find that many of our older manuscripts of the Bible are on parchment.

## The Old Testament

The original Old Testament books were written primarily in Hebrew (still the national language of Israel) with a few verses in Aramaic (spoken in Syria to this day). The writings that became the books of the Bible started during the era of Moses with the Law Books.

Subsequent men of God, beginning with Joshua, Moses' successor as leader of the Jewish nation, continued to write down the revelations they received from God and to record the events that occurred during their lifetimes.

These events then became the history of the Jewish people. The written history and the revelations became the Old Testament, now also known as the Hebrew Bible.

The last book in the Old Testament was written just over four hundred years before the birth of Christ. History shows that there were twenty-two original Old Testament books. Without changing any of the content, some of the longer books were divided and became 1 and 2 Chronicles, 1 and 2 Kings, and so on, so the final number of Old Testament books became thirty-nine.

In one of his later writings, Flavius Josephus, a Jewish secular historian (AD 37–100), wrote,

> We do not possess myriads of inconsistent books, conflicting with each other. Our books, those which are accredited, are but twenty-two and contain the record of all time. Of these, five are the books of Moses, comprising the laws and traditional history from the birth of man down to the death of the lawgiver. This period falls only a little short of three thousand years. From the death of Moses until (King) Artaxerxes (464–424 BC) … the prophets subsequent to Moses wrote the history of the events of their own times in thirteen books. The remaining four books [5 + 13 + 4 = 22]

contain hymns to God and precepts for the conduct of human life.

As the nation chosen by God to be his people, the Israelite had a very special esteem for scripture. As stated by Josephus,

> We have given practical proof of our reverence for our own Scriptures. For although such long ages have now passed, no one has ventured either to add, or to remove, or to alter a syllable; and it is an instinct with every Jew, from the day of his birth, to regard them as the decrees of God, to abide by them, and if need be, cheerfully to die for them.

Josephus wrote that from Artaxerxes to his present day [424 BC to approximately AD 95], "The complete history has been written but has not been deemed worthy of equal credit with the earlier records, because of the failure of the exact succession of the prophets." This reference is to the writings now known as the apocryphal books, which are not a part of the original Bible's sixty-six books. Some of these apocryphal books are valued for their historical information but do not rise to the level of credibility of the Bible's other books.

As previously mentioned, the original writings were in Hebrew with some Aramaic. Since the Greeks established their language as the predominant language of the area, Jewish leaders, in approximately 250 BC, had the original translated into Greek. This translation is known as the Septuagint, meaning "seventy" in Greek, and presumably seventy translators were assigned to the task.

The Hebrew Bible is grouped into three categories.

1. Law Books: Genesis, Exodus, Leviticus, Numbers, and Deuteronomy
2. Prophets: Joshua, Judges, 1 and 2 Samuel, 1 and 2 Kings, Isaiah, Jeremiah, Ezekiel, and the book of the Twelve.

3. Writings: Psalms, Proverbs, Job, Song of Solomon, Ruth, Lamentations, Ecclesiastes, Esther, Daniel, Ezra, Nehemiah, and 1 and 2 Chronicles.

The Old Testament Canon was established prior to the birth of Christ. The word *canon* is traced to the Greek *kanon*, a "reed" that was used as a measuring rod and later evolved into a standard or rule. This standard was applied to the list of books that were *received* (Latin: *receptus)* as holy scripture. It is important to understand that the authority of a book is inherent in that book; when a book is canonized, we recognize the authority of the book, we do not give it authority by canonizing it.

In the New Testament, Jesus and the apostles continually referred to the holy scriptures in their messages. When they stated "it is written," there was no question about what they were referring to. Jesus gave us a clear understanding as to what he considered the extent of scripture when speaking about biblical martyrs: "from the blood of Abel to the blood of Zechariah who perished between the altar and the sanctuary" (Luke 11:51).

The first martyr was Abel, early in the book of Genesis, when he was slain by his brother Cain. The last martyr in the Old Testament was Zechariah (2 Chronicles 24:20–21). Although in the current Old Testament, the last book is Malachi, in the original Hebrew Bible, Chronicles was the last of the twenty-two books. There can be but one interpretation of Christ's intention that martyrdom occurred throughout the scriptures from the very beginning to the very end. Is there any higher authority as to the validity of the original canon?

Several renowned early church fathers confirmed the validity of the Old Testament canon. In the third century, Origen (AD 185–254) named each of the twenty-two Old Testament books. Origen was known as a first-rate Christian philosopher and author of the first exposition of Christian theology. Another well-known church father was Jerome (AD 345–420). Jerome was a very active and outspoken church leader. Pope Damasus commissioned him in

385 to translate the Bible into the scholarly language of the period, Latin. Twenty-three years later, he completed the translation that became known as the Latin Vulgate. His translation was the only approved translation well into the sixteenth century and is still the official Latin translation of the Roman Catholic Church. In his Latin translation, Jerome included the Apocrypha in an addendum, but he made it clear they were "church books" and not qualified to be in the inspired canon.

The Apocrypha is a collection of books that generally were written in the period beginning approximately 400 BC to as late as AD 200. *Apocrypha* comes from the Greek word for "hidden" or "secretive"; it also came to mean a book whose origin was unknown. Generally, when the apocryphal books are referenced, we normally refer to the fourteen or fifteen (the "or" is because in certain references, one of the books, Baruch, is included in the Letter of Jeremiah) books, most of which were written between the Old and New Testaments, hence they are sometimes referred to as the intertestamental books.

Some of these books are very well written and serve a very useful purpose as historical references that help us understand the everyday concerns, problems, tribulations, and lifestyles of the Jewish people of the period, especially when there was a lack of information provided between the two testaments. However, due to the doubtful origins of these books, the inconsistencies between them and scripture, and the almost total lack of spiritual references to any of these books by Jesus or the apostles, there had been a virtual unanimity from all that they should not be considered for inclusion in the canon.

Throughout church history, its leaders often acknowledged the usefulness of the Apocrypha, but they consistently rejected elevating them to the status of authoritative scripture. Many reasons were cited.

- These books were never included in the Hebrew canon of the Hebrew Bible; the Jews never accepted the Apocrypha as God-given scripture. They understood that the Old Testament was a collection of Jewish history and law.

- There is no evidence that Jesus and the apostles accepted these books as scripture.
- They contain many errors and contradictions to the Old Testament and offer no evidence or signs of inspiration.
- Early church fathers such as Origen and Jerome (the translator of the Latin Vulgate) did not include or support the inclusion of these books as divine scripture.

Yet, on April 8, 1546, almost two thousand years after the Hebrew Bible was canonized, the Roman Catholic Church pronounced the Old Testament Apocrypha as authoritative and canonical scripture at the Council of Trent. The council also decreed that the Latin Vulgate was the only authentic scripture and that the "Holy Mother Church" was the only true interpreter of scripture.

The fifteen books of the Apocrypha are

1. The First Book of Esdras
2. The Second Book of Esdras
3. The Letter of Jeremiah
4. Prayer of Azariah and the Song of Three Young Men
5. Tobit
6. Susanna
7. Judith
8. Bel and the Dragon
9. The Additions to the Book of Esther
10. The Prayer of Manasseh
11. The Wisdom of Solomon
12. The First Book of Maccabees
13. The Second Book of Maccabees
14. Ecclesiasticus, or the Wisdom of Jesus the Son of Sirach
15. Baruch (Sometimes included in the Letter of Jeremiah)

All these books (with the exception of the 1 and 2 Esdras and the Prayer of Manasseh) were canonized by the Roman Catholic Church and are now known as the deuterocanonical (*deuteros* is Greek for second) books. The Catholic Bible now has forty-six Old Testament books. Five of the above books were merged into previously existing Old Testament books. The Catholic New Testament did not change or incorporate any apocryphal material; it kept the original twenty-seven books.

## The New Testament

It is generally accepted that the New Testament was written in Greek. As with the Old Testament, some verses are in Aramaic. Since Greek was the predominant language of the area, there was no need for a translation of the New Testament until Pope Damasus commissioned Jerome to translate it into Latin in the late fourth century. Jerome eventually translated both the Old and New Testaments into what became known as the Latin Vulgate; this translation is still in use by the Roman Catholic Church.

Scholars generally agree that the books of the New Testament were written in a fifty-year period, with the first one being written some twenty years after the crucifixion of Jesus. There is general agreement that 1 Corinthians, authored by the apostle Paul, was the first New Testament book written, while the gospel of Mark written by John Mark (the apostle Peter's assistant) was the first of the Gospels. The last book is generally attributed to the apostle John while he was imprisoned by the Roman emperor on the island of Patmos. This last book, Revelation, was written late in the first century.

It is important to repeat that the writers of the New Testament, as was the case with the authors of the Old Testament books, lived during the period they wrote about and participated in or witnessed the events (or had first-person corroboration of the events) included in their books. One of the corroborated events was when Luke wrote about the birth of Jesus and the events surrounding that birth; evidence suggests that Jesus' mother provided the information in Luke's account.

Furthermore, many other witnesses to those events were still alive after these books were written; the record shows no disagreements with any of the recorded events.

We have established that the eight authors of the New Testament were highly reputable men. Four of the writers were apostles—Peter, John, Matthew, and Paul. Of these, Jesus personally appeared to and selected Paul as an apostle. The other three walked with and were taught by Jesus personally throughout his ministry on earth. Two of the authors (Luke and John Mark) were mentored by apostles. Luke was the apostle Paul's personal physician and aide. Mark was mentored by the apostle Peter. Tradition has it that the upper room, the place where Jesus observed the Last Supper, was in Mark's house. The final two authors were none other than two of Jesus' four brothers, James and Jude.

As is the Old Testament, the New Testament is grouped into categories.

1. The five history books: Matthew, Mark, Luke, John, and the Acts of the Apostles. The first four books listed are also known as the Gospels, with Matthew, Mark, and Luke also known as the synoptic Gospels because of their similarity (Greek *sun*, "together," and *opsis*, "seeing").
2. The twenty-one books of doctrine: Romans, 1 and 2 Corinthians, Galatians, Ephesians, Philippians, Colossians, 1 and 2 Thessalonians, 1 and 2 Timothy, Titus, Philemon, Hebrews, James, 1 and 2 Peter, 1, 2, and 3 John, and Jude.
3. The book of prophecy: Revelation.

### The Canon of the New Testament

After Jesus' ascension, the church continued to use the Old Testament as its book of scripture. The church's members probably had no thoughts of new writings. Yet a few short years after Christ, to stay in touch with and provide guidance to newly established churches, the apostles, most notably Paul, began to write long, detailed letters to new believers. These letters were passed on from one new congregation to another. The information in these letters spoke with such a clear authority and was of such universal application that before they were worn out, scribes would copy them and continue their circulation. Some of the other apostles or their aides also wrote to their churches and often would reduce some of their sermons and their experiences to writing. These too were circulated, copied, and recopied.

The apostle Peter recognized early in his ministry that these letters were not just correspondence; they were special and were to be paid attention to and treasured. In 2 Peter 2:15, he wrote,

> Bear in mind that our Lord's patience means salvation, just as our dear brother Paul also wrote you with the wisdom that God gave him. He writes the same way in all of his letters … His letters contain some things that are hard to understand, which ignorant and unstable people distort, as they do the other Scriptures, to their own destruction.

In essence, he compared Paul's letters to other scripture.

Just before his ascension, Christ told his apostles that after he left, he would send the Holy Spirit, who would remind them of everything he had taught them so they could be his witnesses "in Jerusalem, and in all of Judea and Samaria, and to the ends of the earth" (Acts 1:8). So there can be no doubt that Jesus' teachings to his apostles were indeed intended to add to the established scripture.

Scholars estimate that as many as 2,000 books were pretenders for inclusion in the New Testament. Yet throughout the various churches, more often than not, the same twenty-two to twenty-seven books were being used, and they were authoritative in and of themselves.

Nonetheless, a few "notable" leaders sometimes injected some of their personal interpretations into some of these books and would try to create their own list of the authoritative books. Marcion was one of these leaders. In the late second century, he generated a list of books he proclaimed as the new authoritative list. He felt that the God of old (Old Testament) and the new God were not the same. The old God was "mean," while the new God was "good." Therefore, any book that did not agree with this concept was excluded, while any book that agreed with him was of course included. Church fathers would soon voice concern over some of these would-be authoritative lists.

Notwithstanding these challenges, the authoritative books continued to gain respect and acceptance throughout the church. The first known listing of these books is known as the Muratoriam Fragment it dates from the middle to latter second century. It includes all the books in the New Testament except Hebrews, James, 1 and 2 Peter, and 3 John. Noteworthy is the inclusion of the Wisdom of Solomon and the Apocalypse of Peter with the caveat, "some of our people do not want to have them read in church."

In the third century, Origen provided a listing of these books, and his list was the same as the Muratorium Fragment. However, Origen later included the five previously excluded books to make his list the same as the one we now use. Roman Emperor Constantine, having declared Christianity the Roman religion, convened a church council in AD 325. One of his main goals was to ensure the unity of the church and avoid fragmentation. What to include in the New Testament was discussed in great detail, but the final canonization was not to occur until some seventy years later.

In AD 367, another church father, Athanasius (AD 296–376) published a list of books that is the same as the one we use today. Finally, in AD 397, at the Council of Carthage, the twenty-seven books of the New Testament were accepted in *receptus*, that is, "as received" from divine authority, and recognizing that authority, the church canonized the New Testament.

The authority of scripture is not derived from anyone or any human institution; all authority is inherent in scripture; we can do naught but recognize it. The canon is a list of authoritative books; it is not an authoritative list of books. Perhaps it would be easier to understand this concept if we consider the music of Beethoven and Mendelssohn. Their music is great because our sensitivities tell us it is, not because some self-proclaimed group of experts says it is.

### The "Other" Books

Earlier, we saw there were many other books (sometimes referred to as the New Testament Apocrypha) that were not included in the New Testament canon. Many of these books were written from a Gnostic (Greek *gnostos*, "known") perspective. The Gnostics believed that you had to have a special, mystical knowledge to be given eternal life and that the Gnostics had and controlled that knowledge. These books were very obvious frauds and were for the most part easily proven as such.

Yet there remain those who grasp at most anything to "prove" the fallibility of scripture. The recent movie *Stigmata* comes to mind; in it are claims that the church had gone to great extremes, even murder, to keep the gospel of Thomas from becoming public because this "gospel" showed that material things (buildings, land, material wealth) were not necessary to worship God. That truism is in many of the Old and New Testament books. The supposed gospel of Thomas was not included for a myriad of reasons, not the least of which was that the apostle Thomas could not have written it because evidence shows that it was written in the second century AD. Yes, it is and was a fraud.

Of these other books, two are noteworthy: the Shepherd of Hermes and Clements. These two books are well written and have a wealth of good, insightful information. Tradition has it that although they were considered contenders for inclusion, the authors excluded themselves because they felt they could not measure up to apostolic authority.

## Is Our Bible the Same as the Original?

History shows us that when we humans try to convince others of something we strongly believe true, we often have a propensity to unknowingly or perhaps knowingly skew corroborating information into that which best supports our beliefs. That being true, how can we know with any reasonable assurance that, having accepted that the originals reflected events as they happened, subsequent copiers and translators might not have embellished the writings to enhance the storyline?

That is a valid question. We know that the original New Testament writings were probably written on material that had a short life, more than likely papyrus rolls. And, as mentioned earlier, because of their relatively short life, the material had to be copied frequently. This led to many copies being made and carried to many churches, many countries, and literally throughout the world.

### The Witnesses

The simple necessity of making many copies has been a major factor in the objective testability of many facets of scripture. You can take a "witness" (a copy or part of a copy from as far back as the first or second century BC) and compare it to a current copy in Romania,

Canada, or South America. You will find the message is the same. This huge number of copies is also useful in finding textual "errors."

Christians are indeed fortunate in that we have literally thousands of witnesses available to us to use as comparisons to modern translations. Of these, there are three in the flagship category— really significant witnesses. These manuscripts are written on vellum (a processed leather) which is, of course, much more durable. These witnesses are

- The Vatican Manuscript. This witness includes most of the Bible and dates to the fourth century. It is at the Vatican in Rome and has been there at least since 1481. The Vatican library was established in 1448. This witness is considered the earliest and most complete of the three. Its 759 pages are in Greek and still legible. The Vatican did not allow unsupervised access to its manuscript until 1890, when a complete photographic facsimile was made available to scholars. There was a brief period when the manuscript left the hands of the Vatican in the late 1700s; Napoleon took the manuscript as spoils of war, but it was returned in 1815.

- The Sinaitic Manuscript. In AD 550, Emperor Justinian built the Monastery of St. Catharine at the base of Mount Sinai. In 1844, Constantin von Tischendorf journeyed to the monastery in search of an ancient manuscript rumored to have been there. He discovered it, and many years later, in 1869, he purchased the manuscript and brought it back to Russia. Britain bought the manuscript in 1933, and it now sits on display in the British Library. The Sinaitic Manuscript dates back to the fourth century and is the oldest manuscript with a complete New Testament.

- The Alexandrian Manuscript. Believed to have been copied in Egypt in the fifth century, the manuscript stayed in Alexandria until Cyril Lucar, the Greek patriarch, brought it to Constantinople in the early 1600s. He presented it as a gift to Britain's King Charles I in 1627. Along with the Sinaitic Manuscript, it is displayed in the British Library.

We should note that with little doubt, historically, the most widely read English translation of the Christian Bible has been the King James Version. It was translated from the Latin Vulgate (which was itself translated from the Greek and Hebrew in about 405) and completed in 1611. This translation was completed before any of the three major manuscripts above or any of the large number of subsequent findings was available. The three flagship manuscripts were copied from the Septuagint translation (250 BC) and from the original Greek of the New Testament. We will later discuss some of the variations discovered.

### The Dead Sea Scrolls

Although discoveries of biblical text continue to this day, one of the biggest and most significant finds in recent history has been the discovery of what became known as the Dead Sea Scrolls. The discoveries started in March 1948, when a young Arab looking for a stray goat stumbled onto some earthen jars in a cave. He took some of these jars filled with leather rolls with writing on them. These rolls eventually made their way to Jerusalem and into the hands of Hebrew scholars.

The findings were explosive! The leather rolls were copies of scripture dating back to the first and second centuries BC. These copies predated some of the oldest copies then possessed by four to six hundred years. In addition to copies of scripture, there were other writings describing the lives of the locals in the first and second centuries BC.

Comparisons of these texts to current Old Testament translations show a remarkable consistency. There were some variations that we will discuss later.

## Is the Bible Inerrant?

We now turn our attention to the question of inerrancy. To minimize confusion, we need to make sure we start with the same understanding of some key terms and perhaps clarify some presuppositions. We have heard some people say that the Bible is *infallible*, others say it is *inerrant*, and sometimes the word *inspired* is interjected. We use the word *infallible* when we mean that whatever we are describing is not capable of being wrong. On the other hand, the word *inerrant* means that it is capable of being wrong but it is not.

We need to expand this definition. Inerrancy does not mean with scientific precision; it does mean there are no errors of truth, no fraud, no lies, and in a few instances, allowance is made for literary hyperbole (an exaggeration to emphatically make a point).

A good example of a biblical hyperbole is found in Mark 9:47, in which Jesus was talking about things that might cause us to stumble, to be turned away from God: "And if your eye causes you to stumble, pluck it out. It is better for you to enter the kingdom of God with one eye than to have two eyes and be thrown into hell." Any doubt as to where the emphasis is?

A significant part of Jesus' ministry to the masses was done through stories known as parables (stories with storylines that the masses would be familiar with to make or clarify a point).

When we say the Bible was written by men *inspired* by God, we are making a literal statement. Although the authors wrote their books using their own words and intellects, the substance of the message was God inspired.

So what about this inerrancy? We have seen that the Bible provides true historical value, there is overwhelming evidence of its basic reliability, and it has withstood relentless secular scrutiny; therefore, we can say with complete confidence that if the Bible says that something is true, we must accept it as such.

We need to understand that the assertion of inerrancy applies specifically to the original scriptures. Subsequent copies and translations were by actions of men, not necessarily inspired men. Our subsequent discussion on biblical "errors" addresses this area.

Therefore, we can state with complete confidence that

- the Bible is *inspired* by God, therefore, the Bible is *infallible*,
- the Bible is infallible, therefore, the Bible is *inerrant*, and
- the Bible is inerrant, therefore, the Bible is *true and trustworthy.*

Throughout the New Testament, Jesus stated without equivocation and in many different ways that the Bible was the Word of God, hence inerrant. To some, this may appear to be circular reasoning, because we are using the Bible (quotes from Jesus from the Bible) as proof that the Bible is true and trustworthy.

However, a few chapters earlier in this discussion, we established that in every area that the Bible has been tested, it has been proven true and correct. Having been tested for centuries, and having found no errors that would have any impact on the truth and validity of the Bible, then by the laws of probability and the law of logical inference, we must accept that what the Bible states as true is in fact true.

### Errors and Variations in the Bible

This discussion on biblical errors and variations in no way contradicts the previous section on the inerrancy of the Bible. All of these variations occur in the various copies, and none is considered significant, with the possible exception of one in the book of Mark in the New Testament.

A word on errors and variations: I start this section using both words because more than likely, we have all heard both terms used at one time or another. But for the record, Bible scholars do not normally use the word *errors*, they refer to any inconsistency between copies or translations as a *variation*. For some unknown reason, skeptics are only too willing to use the word *error*. In reality, we do not have the original writings on hand with which to compare any inconsistency; all we do have are variations between copies.

Skeptics readily point out that over 100,000 errors have been found in the New Testament text. What they don't point out is that there are over 4,000 different manuscripts, and if each had the same variation, it would only take twenty-five variations plus one to exceed the 100,000.

Let's take a look at some of these variations and their significance. Scholars categorize variations into three categories: trivial, significant but with no consequences, and significant with possible consequences.

### Trivial Variations

The overwhelming number of variations falls into this category. They include such errors as inserting the word *and* when an older manuscript omits it; addition of the words "to hear" at the end of a scripture that reads, "the one who has ears, to hear"; addition or omission of the words *the* and *for*; different spellings for names; some manuscripts read the "birth of Jesus" while another has "the birth of Christ," and other such minor variations. Most of these variations are so insignificant that newer translations normally will not even footnote the variation(s) in their versions. Yet every one of these variations is counted and tabulated.

Although the specifics of counting, tabulating, and selecting between variations is not within the purview of this endeavor, we should, however, note that when biblical scholars come upon a variation between manuscripts, they will select the most awkward one. They assume the variation that puts the topic in the least favorable light is the one most likely to be correct. This rule has served them well.

### Significant Variations with No Consequences

These variations, as the name implies, are not necessarily trivial, but their inclusion or exclusion from scripture is easily ascertained by comparison of various manuscripts. Here, the rule is basically that the older the manuscript, the higher its propensity for accuracy.

John 7:53 to 8:11 is a good example of this type of variation. This is the story of the adulterous woman brought to Jesus by the Pharisees to see if he would condemn her: "He who is without sin cast the first stone." All new translations whether they include or omit this scripture footnote that this variation is not included in all major and significant ancient manuscripts and is not normally found in manuscripts until late in the eighth century. The story is a good one and has a good moral lesson, but evidence strongly suggests that it was added to John, probably through church tradition.

Whether this story is included or excluded, it has no impact on the accuracy, truthfulness, or message of the Bible. However, it is a variation and must be noted as such. There are a few other similar variations but they are much less significant than the one cited.

### Significant Variations with Possible Consequences

The only significant variation of note with possible consequences is Mark 16:9–20. This variation is significant because many of the older and newer manuscripts include these verses. However, the problem becomes significant because just as many older and newer manuscripts do not include these verses.

Although there appear to be some inconsistencies in writing styles between the cited verses and the rest of Mark, the basic subject material is consistent with scripture. And since Matthew and/or

Luke also include most of this material in their gospels, whether it is included or excluded from Mark, the biblical message is the same.

## Summary

We have seen how the Bible came to be, how it was written, who wrote it, who their intended audiences were, and how it was finally accepted, i.e., canonized.

The Mormons claim that the Bible was heavily corrupted sometime after the crucifixion and the destruction of the Jewish nation, perhaps late in the first century. The Book of Mormon was given to the prophet John Smith in a very private and special revelation by an angel sent by God in the nineteenth century. This Book of Mormon was the new and reliable word of God; according to Mormons, it was more correct than the corrupted Bible. Is this biblical corruption true or even possible?

The huge number of witnesses available (by last count, we are fast approaching 20,000), some of which date back to at least 125 BC (the Dead Sea Scrolls), shows that without reservation, the scripture in use today is the same as the scripture in use during the time of Jesus' ministry.

The Mormon charge that much of the Bible suffered corruption during the latter part of the first century is without basis. The Dead Sea Scrolls, dating some 225 years before the Bible's corruption was supposed to have occurred, emphatically show that the biblical message is the same now, some 1,900 years after the supposed corruption, as it was 225 years before the supposed corruption. So we can say without reservation or equivocation that yes, the message of the Bible we hold today is the same as the original.

There are no errors or variations in the Bible; there are some variations in the copies and translations of the Bible, but in no way can any of these variations be interpreted as errors in the sense that they prove a fallacy or an untruth in scripture. All the scrutiny, secular research, skeptical analysis, and more-recent torrents of vehemence thrown at the Bible have not altered one iota of its message. It remains as meaningful and as powerful today as the day when it was written.

The majority of those who have had some contact with the Bible or its contents but have made no serious effort to read it almost invariably have a deeply ingrained belief that it is too difficult for the average person to understand. They believe that only those who are properly trained are able to read and correctly understand it.

Granted, for over a thousand years, the church actively discouraged (for much of that period they actually did not allow under penalty of excommunication, torture, or even death) its members from reading the Bible because, in its opinion, the average person was not capable of reading it much less understanding it.

With German and English translations of the Bible and Gutenberg's invention of the printing press, Bibles soon became available to and understandable even by (in accordance with John Wycliffe, 1330–1384, English scholar, theologian, translator, and professor at Oxford University) the common English plowboy. Wycliffe was the first to translate the Latin Vulgate into English.

This accomplishment was vehemently opposed by the church, which said, "By this translation, the Scriptures have become vulgar, and they are more available to lay, and even to women who can read, than they were to learned scholars, who have a high intelligence. So the pearl of the gospel is scattered and trodden underfoot by swine" To which Wycliffe replied, "Englishmen learn Christ's law best in English. Moses heard God's law in his own tongue: so did Christ's apostles." (Pg 210, *131 Christian's Everyone Should Know,* Mark Galli and Ted Olsen)

From a secular perspective, the Bible is a profound literary work because of its detail, accuracy, amazing clarity, and its expansive coverage of its subject from the beginning of the human ability to record history to approximately 100 AD. As impressive as the Bible may be for its historical record, that fact does not hold a candle to its significance as a spiritual anchor for the believer. The Bible explicitly guides the believer through life and into the next life.

An oft-heard concern, especially from new believers, centers around those people they knew who died and never had access to the Bible. Would they be condemned as nonbelievers? The Bible addresses this concern by pointing to God's natural revelation. Every human being is the recipient of God's revelation. No one can say he or she doesn't know of God. Those in the deepest heart of Africa, or on the hot sand dunes of the Sahara, or on the highest mountain in the Himalayas know of God. Because they know of God, they will be held accountable. They know of God because God has shown them his creation. God is not a part of creation; he is its Creator. He has shown them his love and caring through everything he made. This knowledge of God through his creation is known as natural revelation. A review of the first chapter of Romans in the New Testament expands this concept.

In addition to this natural revelation, we are very fortunate God has also given us his special revelation, the Bible. How can we not be at least curious about God's specific guidance?

The Bible is not divided into two separate, distinct parts, i.e., the Old and New Testaments. The Old Testament lays the foundation, and the New Testament builds and expands on that foundation.

Throughout history, God has been providing us with increasing revelation; that is not to say he is giving us new or altered revelation. He builds on the revelation he has already given us. We can best understand this concept by looking at and understanding the seven successive covenants between God and humanity. There are some variations on the study of this concept: dispensationalism (distinct biblical periods in which God deals with humans according to certain divine goals), covenant theology, and new covenant theology.

The word *testament* was selected by church leaders instead of what many consider a more appropriate word, *covenant*. A modern equivalent for *covenant* would be *contract*. As with any contract, a covenant requires at least two parties, God and ...

## *The World's Bestseller*

The oldest books are in the Bible, the first book ever printed was the Bible, and the Bible has been the world's bestseller throughout history. In the United States alone, 26 million Bibles are sold annually (an average of 72,000 per day). By comparison, the top five best sellers combined average annual sales of approximately 12 million. But do people actually read the Bible? Are they influenced by it? Scholars estimate that if all references to the Bible were removed from all the great art and literature of the world, our libraries would shrink by half! You decide if it has had an impact on humanity.

# Chapter 16

## Jesus—A Good Man, a Good Teacher, a Prophet, or God?

Who was Jesus? Was he just a good man, a good teacher, a prophet sent by God to give us some revelation? Or was he (as some claim) God? We have already established that several historians, including Josephus, Pliny the Younger, and Tacitus in the late first and early second centuries wrote about this man called Jesus. From a secular viewpoint, there is no doubt that Jesus existed.

His love in deed and action but even more so in his message certainly established him as a good man. His message of love, service, and humility attested to this goodness. There are no writings that do not speak well of him. Yes, he was a good man.

In his Testimonium Flavianum, Josephus wrote, "About this time there lived Jesus, a wise man ... For he was one who wrought surprising feats and was a teacher of such people as accept the truth gladly. He won over many Jews and many of the Greeks."

The large crowds that gathered to hear his teachings were certainly proof of his abilities as a teacher and to the credibility of his message. His message was credible then, and it is just as credible and appropriate today. Jesus was a good teacher.

Muslims and Jews believe Jesus was a prophet. In the Old Testament, prophets were selected by God to be his voice to the people. If they were men (there were in fact also a few women prophetesses in the Bible) selected by God; they were obviously good men. Jesus was very much a prophet of God.

There seems to be very little disagreement that Jesus was a good man, a good teacher, and a prophet. As a rule, secularists have no problem with the above statement. The problem comes when they realize that this good man and good teacher also claimed to be God; this they cannot accept. Therefore, it follows that if he was not God, he must have been a liar or a psycho. Can a liar or a psycho be a good man or a good teacher? A real conundrum.

### Was Jesus God?

Perhaps he never really said he was God. Could be that religious zealots made that part up. Not so. In the Bible, Jesus was asked if he was the Messiah. Jesus answered, "I and the Father are one" (John 10:30). A little while later, the apostle Philip asked, "Lord, show us the Father and that will be enough for us." Jesus answered, "Anyone who has seen me has seen the Father" (John 14:8, 9). When the Pharisees were telling Jesus they were the chosen ones because they were directly descended from Abraham, Jesus answered, "Before Abraham was, I AM" (John 8:58). There are numerous other direct and clear biblical references that show Jesus was in fact God. But of all the biblical references to Jesus being God, none is more powerful or more beautiful or as direct as is John 1:1, 2, 14, 10, and 11.

> In the beginning was the Word, and the Word was with God, and the Word was God. He was with God in the beginning. The Word became flesh and made his dwelling among us. He was in the world, and though the world was made through him, the world did not recognize him. He came to that which was his own, but his own did not receive him.

In the references above it is clear that the "Word" is Jesus. As beautiful as the above reference is, it also shows humanity's inhumanity to its Creator. He came to help his own creation, but his own did not receive him.

### Prophecies of the Messiah

In addition to the references above supporting his claims of being God, numerous Old Testament prophecies proclaim him as the Messiah. Scholars have estimated that over three hundred Old Testament prophecies concerned the coming Messiah, and not one of them has been shown to be false!

The book of Isaiah is probably the most prolific; Isaiah 53:3–9, 12 is often cited as one of the most astounding. Excerpts from this reference include,

- he was pierced for our transgressions [a Roman soldier lanced his side while on the cross],
- he was crushed for our inequities [he was forced to carry his heavy cross part of the way to his crucifixion site],
- by his wounds we are healed [miracle upon healing miracle has been evidenced],
- he was oppressed and afflicted, yet he did not open his mouth [at his trial, he offered no defense],
- he was cut off from the land of the living [he died on the cross], and
- he was assigned a grave with the wicked and with the rich in his death [he was buried in a new tomb provided by a rich Jewish official].

These are but a few excerpts. We must remember that the book of Isaiah was written over six hundred years before Jesus' death on the cross.

Other prophecies include Micah specifying that the Messiah would be born in Bethlehem and Isaiah predicting he would be born of a virgin. Jeremiah told of his ancestry, and Psalms, in a prediction written by King David, specified how he would die—by crucifixion, with hands and feet pierced. Astoundingly, this prophecy was written over nine hundred years before the Romans had invented death by crucifixion.

Knowing some could claim that it might be possible for somebody to accidentally fulfill these prophecies, I point out that the probability of only eight of these prophecies coming true is one in one hundred million billion, or put another way, if you covered the entire state of Texas two feet deep in silver dollars with only one gold dollar in the mix, to beat the odds given in the figure above, you would have to randomly parachute into these two feet of silver coins and on the first try pick up the gold dollar (no GPS, no radar)!

If you look at accidentally fulfilling forty-eight prophecies, your chances go up so high that if you counted every atom in the universe, you still would not have a number large enough to show the odds.

## The Second Adam

When God created Adam and Eve, he put them in the garden of Eden. There was to be a relationship between God and Adam and Eve in an idyllic, permanent arrangement. Since there was no sin, there was also no death. Humanity was meant never to taste death. However, for the relationship between God and humans to be meaningful, they had to choose to be in the relationship with God. For them to choose, they had to have the choice of either entering the relationship or not; this was free will.

### *Man's Rejection of God's Perfect Plan*

By disobeying God, Adam rejected the arrangement established by God, thereby introducing sin into the world. God, being unable to tolerate sin, separated from Adam and Eve. With the introduction of sin, Adam and Eve introduced death.

Death came in two forms. Death came to the flesh; it would decay and cease to be. In the second death, humans' souls (which exist forever) would be condemned to eternal separation from God in an exceedingly unpleasant way.

## The Destruction of Sin and the Rebirth

God provided the means by which humanity could reestablish this relationship and avoid the pains of the second death. The first death was the consequence of sin and was, therefore, unavoidable. However, the rapid degeneration of humanity continued until total debauchery, immorality, and idol worship became the norm.

God chose to destroy sinful humanity with the exception of the one good man and his family, Noah. This family was to carry the seed of humanity into the future. The flood gave humanity a new start as Noah's family began the repopulation of earth.

## Israel: The Chosen Nation of Priests

It was not long before humanity began to sink into its past sinful lifestyle that God chose Abraham to lead a new nation of priests that would be the catalyst to lead humanity back to God. This new nation, Israel, was to consist of the chosen of God, who were provided guidance and instructions on how to reestablish the lost relationship. The means for the reestablishment of this relationship, though clear and specific, were more often than not attempted by people half-heartedly if at all.

The means by which humanity was to be forgiven was by seeking forgiveness, the spilling of blood (through specific rituals, the rabbi would transfer the sins of the repentant onto an unblemished animal, the animal would be sacrificed, and the blood of the animal would wash away his sins), and obeying God's commandments.

As time went on, humanity, for the most part, continued in its sinful ways. Wars, captivity, droughts, famine, and other hardships often brought people closer to God, but times of prosperity and plenty more often than not would see them drifting away again.

Whereas Adam was the one man who had brought sin to humanity, the sin that had brought the world to near total depravity (man had shown that on his own he was not capable of breaking this sin cycle), another Adam was needed who could break this sin cycle. This new Adam had to be without sin so he could take on the sin humanity had not been able to control, and he had to be an unblemished, perfect sacrifice to satisfy the requirement for the shedding of blood to complete the atonement. By the shedding of his blood, he would take on the sins of the world. This second Adam was Jesus.

## The Trinity

A central part of the Christian belief is monotheism, the belief in one God. The Ten Commandments God gave Moses had as its first commandment, "You shall have no other Gods before me" (Exodus 20:3). The early church fathers had some difficulty with the one-God concept since the Bible also spoke of Jesus as God and the Holy Spirit as God. This difficulty persisted for many years.

The concept of the Trinity evolved, though it still had difficulties for not just the average person but also for biblical scholars of the time to understand and rationalize it. The actual word *Trinity* is not mentioned in the Bible. The concept, however, is mentioned in various degrees of specificity throughout both the Old and New Testaments. The earliest reference to what we now know as the Trinity is in Genesis 1:26: "Then God said let *us* make mankind in *our* image, in *our* likeness" (my emphasis). The plural pronouns in this reference clearly show the presence of more than one "person" in this discussion.

With the adoption of the Nicene Creed in AD 325, the concept of the Trinity reached general acceptance, and by the end of the same century, the Trinity was ensconced in church doctrine in its current form. The Trinity is one God in three persons, God the Father, Son, and Holy Spirit.

Though the definition appears clear and understandable, the concept stretches the mind. We will probably never truly understand this concept in this life, but we accept it on faith.

## Summary

We have seen that Jesus was a good man, slow to anger, quick to love, and indeed very patient and understanding. He was an exceptional teacher. His message and his ever-increasing number of followers attest to his special abilities as a teacher. He was indeed a prophet. His ministry showed his special knowledge of scripture and connection to God the Father. He was all this, but most important, he was the promised Messiah of scripture.

All these qualities made him the perfect, sinless man, one qualified to correct the shortcomings of Adam, who had introduced sin into the world. He would in fact become the second Adam, but this time, he would take sin unto himself and enable us to overcome the deadly effects of sin.

We also reviewed the Christian concept become the doctrine of the Trinity. Though it is hard to comprehend and fully understand, it is a very central and important concept of Christianity.

# Chapter 17

# The Gospels: Matthew, Mark, Luke, and John

Gospel literally means *good news*. But good news of what, for what, from what? To better understand and define the phrase, we need to recap some of the history leading up to the gospel.

## The Covenants

### The Adamic Covenant

From the very beginning, God sought a relationship with humanity that would have guidelines and a certain structure. The guidelines were called covenants. We have mentioned that a covenant is a contract, and contracts have at least two parties that agree to do something. God's agreement with Adam was that he was to live in the garden of Eden, was to be a steward of the things on earth, have dominion over all living creatures, and with his wife, Eve, was to populate the world. In return, Adam was to be obedient to God.

In his first major test, not to eat from the Tree of Knowledge of Good and Evil, Adam failed; he broke the covenant. By eating from the forbidden tree, he not only broke the covenant, he also rejected the personal relationship with God.

### The Abrahamic Covenant

The next major covenant was with Abram (God later renamed him Abraham). Abram was seventy-five when God told him, "I will make you into a great nation, and I will bless you … I will bless those who bless you, and whoever curses you I will curse; and all peoples on earth will be blessed through you" (Genesis 12:2, 3). This had to be a fantastic proposition for Abram; his end of the covenant was just to obey God. However, there was reason for Abraham to be skeptical about God's promise. He and his wife were childless. How would God make him into a great nation without a son? His wife was surely barren.

Still, his faith served him well because he waited, and waited, and waited some more. Yes, there were some problems, some doubts, but he hung in there. At the age of one hundred, some twenty-five years after God initiated the covenant (Sarah was then ninety), his wife conceived and gave birth to Isaac. Abraham did not break the covenant, and God continued the covenant through his offspring.

### The Mosaic Covenant

In Exodus, God, Moses, and the Israelites confirmed the covenant, Moses received the tablets of stone with the commandments written by God. The law was given to Moses over time. The law was quite extensive and covered almost every facet of daily Israeli life. Included in the law were instructions on hygiene, medical procedures, diet, worship, and among others, very specific instructions on the tabernacle, the central place of worship. The Mosaic Law includes some 613 very specific laws.

### The Tabernacle

During the forty-year exodus from Egypt, God instructed Moses to build a tabernacle. Since they were traveling, the tabernacle was designed to be portable. As the place of worship, the tabernacle was erected in the center of each encampment with the twelve tribes camped around it. Every item in the tabernacle was identified in the Bible, including its purpose, the material it was to be made of, and its placement in the tabernacle. This specificity is carried over to the tabernacle itself; its material, color, height, dimensions, and widths were stated. The tabernacle consisted of a walled-in, open-air courtyard (approximately a quarter of an American football field) with a tent of worship inside the courtyard. In the open courtyard were the main sacrificial altar, the sacrificial preparatory tables, and the wash basin.

The tent of worship was divided into two sections: the outer section was the holy place, where priests would conduct worship services, and the inner section was the holy of holies, which was veiled off from the holy place with a heavy curtain. The holy of holies, as God's earthly abode, was indeed sacred, and only the high priest could enter it, and then only once a year to ask for the forgiveness of sins for the people of Israel and to bring an offering of blood. This day was known as the Day of Atonement; we now know it as Yom Kippur.

In the holy of holies was the Ark of the Covenant. Within the ark were the three items most precious to the Israelites: the tablets of the Ten Commandments, Aaron's (Moses' brother and the first high priest) staff with the leaves that had miraculously sprouted from it, and a piece of manna, like those they ate during the exodus.

After the Jews settled in their promised land, the tabernacle remained portable until 957 BC, when King Solomon finished building the permanent temple, still following God's specific guidance. In 587 BC, the Babylonians defeated Judah, took a large portion of the Jewish people captive, and destroyed the temple. Some seventy years later after the exile, the temple was rebuilt more modestly than Solomon's temple, but nevertheless, the Jews had their worship place again.

Around 19 BC, King Herod the Great began a renovation of the temple. This magnificent temple was completed around AD 64, only to be destroyed by the Romans in AD 70. "Jesus left the temple and was walking away when his disciples came up to him to call his attention to its buildings. 'Do you see all these things?' he asked. 'Truly I tell you, not one stone here will be left on another, every one will be thrown down'" (Matthew 24:1–2). And so it was. Jesus said this about forty years earlier.

Since the time of Moses, the temple has always been central to the Jewish religion. Although it has not been rebuilt, Bible prophecy has some very specific things to say about it, so we've not yet heard the last of the temple.

### Other Covenants

In addition to the covenants noted, there were several other covenants that were invariably broken by man. God continually sent his prophets to remind the people of the consequences of not abiding by these covenants and thus disobeying God. The ceremonial worshipping, the atonement requiring individual and recurring sacrifices, the separateness of God from his worshippers (for example, the holy of holies separate from the worship area), the ever-increasing church rites and traditions, the Ten Commandments, and the never-ending requirements of the Mosaic Law were simply not producing the desired results. Something new had to be introduced.

### Proclamation of a New Covenant

Around 650 BC, the prophet Jeremiah gave us an indication of what was to come.

> "The days are coming," declares the Lord "when I will make a new covenant with the people of Israel and with the people of Judah. It will not be like the covenant I made with their ancestors when I took them by the hand to lead them out of Egypt, because they broke my covenant, though I was a husband to them," declares the

Lord. "This is the covenant I will make with the people of Israel after that time" declares the Lord, "I will put my law in their minds and write it on their hearts, I will be their God and they will be my people. No longer will they teach their neighbor or say to one another, 'Know the Lord' because they will all know me, from the least of them to the greatest," declares the Lord. "For I will forgive their wickedness and will remember their sins no more." (Jeremiah 31:31–34)

## The Good News

The prophet Jeremiah pretty well spells out the effect of the good news. All the people will have a knowledge and understanding of the difference between right and wrong. By complying with the new covenant, they will know the Lord will forgive their wickedness and will remember their sins no more through the gospel of Jesus.

## Birth of Jesus

The gospel of Jesus starts with a visit from the angel Gabriel to Mary. The angel, seeing her apprehension, said,

> Do not be afraid, Mary; you have found favor with God. You will conceive and give birth to a son, and you are to call him Jesus. He will be great and will be called the Son of the Most High. The Lord God will give him the throne of his father David, and he will reign over Jacob's descendants forever; his kingdom will never end. (Luke 1:30–33)

With his incarnate (in the flesh) but unheralded birth in the little village of Bethlehem, the angel Gabriel's words were fulfilled. Why was it necessary for Jesus to be born of a virgin? Because of the fall, all humanity has been born with a sin nature. If Jesus had not been born of a virgin, the seed of man would have passed this sin nature on to the baby Jesus and he would have been born a sinner. A man of sin would not have fulfilled the requirement of an unblemished sacrifice.

The good news starts with the birth of Jesus and goes on to his ascension into heaven.

## The Deity of Christ

The manner in which Jesus was born surely attested to his uniqueness. Although the birth gives many real problems to skeptics, the deity of Christ is something the unbeliever cannot accept. The deity of Christ is simply that when he came incarnate (Latin *incarnate*, "made flesh") he was literally God in the flesh. Christ was fully God and fully man. Though it flows easily from the tongue, this concept has momentous implications that make it almost incomprehensible. The Christ, the maker of all that ever was and ever will be, came to earth and took the form of a regular person with all the frailties, feelings, and emotions of a man. He felt hunger, pain, love, and sorrow. He came to be one of us!

The apostle John was very clear and emphatic that to achieve eternal life, we had to be believers. Although many claim to be followers of Christ, many are pretenders, not true believers. How can you tell true believers from deceivers and pretenders? The apostle stated in 1 John 4:1–3, 4,

> Dear friends, do not believe every spirit, but test the spirits to see whether they are from God, because many false prophets have gone out into the world. This is how you can recognize the Spirit of God: Every spirit that acknowledges that Jesus Christ has come in the flesh is from God, but every spirit that does not acknowledge Jesus is not from God … You, dear children are from

God and have overcome them, because the one who is in
you is greater than the one who is in the world.

Although this test seems to be overly simplistic, if we just look
around at all the other non-Christian religions and see how they
view Jesus, perhaps we can *test* the test. Muslims say that Jesus
was a prophet and a good one at that but most definitely not God.
Mormons state that Jesus was a good man, but he was like us.
Judaism says Jesus was a good teacher but certainly not God. I can
think of no other religion that accepts Jesus as God, especially a God
that became man to atone for our sins. Although the test is hard, it is
indeed effective: if you don't accept the deity of Christ, you are not
from God. This is called denying the incarnation of Jesus Christ.

## The Ministry of Jesus

### The Baptism

When he was thirty, Jesus was baptized by John the Baptist.
Prior to John the Baptist, the "baptismal" ceremony was very
different. Gentiles who wanted to become Jews were required to
publicly read and accept the Jewish scriptures and laws as their own,
undergo circumcision, and finally, since they were not descendants
of Abraham, thus not one of the chosen, they had to undergo a ritual
cleansing, a public bathing to wash away the "Gentile." They would
then be considered Jews.

Thus for a Jew (especially for a Sadducee, one of the ruling
class in the temple, or a Pharisee, a priest or leader in the temple),
a descendant of Abraham, to be told he had to be baptized would
have been an insult, a literal slap in the face because as the chosen,
they were already clean.

Baptism for followers of Christ symbolized the washing away of
sins and death of the flesh by submersion in the water with a rebirth

of the spirit by the emergence from the water. It was also a public statement that the person was then a follower of Christ.

Clearly, sinless Jesus chose to be baptized to symbolically show unity with believers, to humble himself, and to proclaim the start of his public ministry. The moment Jesus came up out of the water, "heaven opened up and the spirit of God descended like a dove and alighted on him. And a voice from heaven said, 'This is my Son, whom I love; in him I am well pleased'" (Matthew 3:16–17).

### The Temptation of Christ

Immediately after his baptism, Jesus went into the desert to fast and prepare himself for ministry. After forty days and forty nights of fasting and preparation, Satan appeared to him, and in his state of hunger and depravation, he tempted Jesus with food, power, and riches. With direct quotes from scripture, Jesus rebuffed each one of Satan's temptations. "Then the devil left him, and angels came and attended him" (Matthew 4:11).

### Jesus Selects His Apostles

Jesus made Capernaum, a small village in northern Israel by the Sea of Galilee, his home, and he ventured from there on his ministry. On an early walk by the Sea of Galilee, he saw Simon (Peter) and Andrew, two brothers, and called them to follow him. A little farther on, he saw James and John, also brothers; he called them, and they also responded. Not one of the twelve apostles hesitated in the slightest when he asked them to follow him. This was certainly an attestation to his persona and a precursor of things to come.

Early in his ministry, Jesus left no doubt that he had come not to abolish the Law (the law requiring sacrifice for atonement or the commandments) or the prophets but to fulfill them. "For truly I tell you, until heaven and earth disappear, not the smallest letter, not the least stroke of a pen, will by any means disappear from the Law until everything is accomplished" (Matthew 5:18).

## The Message

His message of humility, giving to the needy, and love resounded with all who heard it. He said, "You have heard that it was said, 'Love your neighbor and hate your enemy.' But I tell you, love your enemies and pray for those who persecute you" (Matthew 5:43–44). This was somewhat different from the message most had heard and certainly not what the Jewish leaders wanted to hear from one many were calling the Messiah.

A large part of Jesus' ministry was presented in parables (basically telling a story that his listeners could easily understand to make points about his ministry). Such a story would be the one known as the parable of the sower.

> A farmer went out to sow his seed. As he was scattering the seed, some fell along the path, and the birds came and ate it up. Some fell on rocky places, where it did not have much soil. It sprang up quickly, because the soil was shallow. But when the sun came up, the plants were scorched, and they withered because they had no root.
>
> Other seed fell among the thorns, which grew up and choked the plants. Still other seed fell on good soil, where it produced a crop--a hundred, sixty, or thirty times what was sown. (Matthew 13:3–9)

Jesus later explained to his apostles the meaning of the parable.

> When anyone hears the message about the kingdom and does not understand it, the evil one comes and snatches

away what was sown in their heart. This is the seed sown along the path.

The seed falling on rocky ground refers to someone who hears the word and at once receives it with joy. But since they have no root, they last only a short time. When trouble or persecution comes because of the word, they quickly fall away.

The seed falling among the thorns refers to someone who hears the word, but the worries of this life and the deceitfulness of wealth choke the word, making it unfruitful.

But the seed falling on good soil refers to someone who hears the word and understands it. This is the one who produces a crop yielding a hundred, sixty or thirty times what was sown. (Matthew 13:19–23)

To emphasize a point, Jesus sometimes used hyperbole; an example is in Matthew 12:46–50. Jesus was talking to a crowd and was told his mother and brothers were standing outside, wanting to speak to him. He replied, "Who is my mother and who are my brothers?" Pointing to his disciples, he said, "Here are my mother and my brothers. For whoever does the will of my Father in heaven is my brother and sister and mother." There is no doubt that Jesus loved his mother dearly, but his point was that nothing, not even your mother, brothers, or sisters, should stand in the way of worshipping God. He left no doubt; he made his point emphatically.

Jesus' ministry, both in his message and the many healings and miracles he performed, continued to grow and had a tremendous impact on all who heard it—all except the Sadducees and Pharisees, who were more interested in holding on to their power and high standings in the nation of Israel.

### *Trouble with Church Leaders*

Jesus continued to emphasize that the church leaders should give up their traditions and rules and get back to scripture; it was their traditions (which did not adhere to or comply with scripture) that kept them from the kingdom of God. They had often supplemented and contradicted the scriptures with their own rules and regulations; these were the rules of people, not of God. He emphasized this in Mark 7:6–9.

> Isaiah was right when he prophesied about you hypocrites, as it is written: "These people honor me with their lips, but their hearts are far from me. They worship me in vain; their teachings are merely human rules. You have let go of the commands of God and are holding on to human traditions ... You have a fine way of setting aside the commands of God in order to observe your own traditions!"

If they did not change their ways, he clearly told them, they would be condemned. He concluded his vitriolic criticism of the teachers of the law and the Pharisees with "You snakes! You brood of vipers! How will you escape being condemned to hell?" (Matthew 23:33). They could not tolerate being ridiculed and criticized by an upstart, and they began to look for ways to kill him.

## The Passion of Christ

For some time, Jesus had been telling his apostles that the day was coming when he would be turned over to the leaders, who would torture and kill him. They apparently were not able to comprehend this until the third time he told them.

The three years of Jesus' ministry were coming to a close. He knew he had to die as a sacrifice for humanity. You do not change

God's law, you fulfill it. The Law required the shedding of blood for the atonement of sin.

Jesus and his disciples journeyed to Jerusalem to celebrate Passover. His disciples, knowing what the leaders of the temple were capable of, tried to talk Jesus into perhaps not going that time, but Jesus knew what he had to do.

As we start discussing the Passion Week, it would be helpful to understand that in Jesus' time on earth, the Jewish day was a twenty-four-hour period that started at six in the evening. The Jewish Sabbath, Saturday, started at six Friday evening and ended at six Saturday evening. Additionally, a part of any day would be counted as a full day.

### The Week of the Passion

Jesus and his disciples arrived in Jerusalem on the Sunday before Passover. As he had humbly entered this world in a stable with only shepherds to welcome him, he so entered Jerusalem as the "King of the Jews" on a lowly donkey. Though his arrival was humble, his welcome was not. A huge, loud, boisterous crowd paid him tribute. Palm fronds, coats, shawls, and other tribute were laid in front of his path. Loud and vociferous adulation, with shouts of Hosanna, was heard throughout Jerusalem. It was so loud that the Pharisees implored him to rebuke and quiet the crowd. "I tell you," Jesus replied, "if they keep quiet, the stones will cry out" (Matthew 19:40).

Jesus visited the temple and left Jerusalem to spend the night with friends in Bethany, a short distance from Jerusalem.

On the following morning, Monday, Jesus went to the temple. Seeing all the commerce taking place in the temple courtyard, he became highly agitated. He started releasing birds, overturning tables, and driving out the merchants. At the top of his voice, he yelled, "It is written ... My house will be a house of prayer, but you have made it a den of robbers" (Luke 19:46). The Sadducees and

Pharisees were highly troubled because this was a huge source of income for them. They took note.

On Tuesday, Jesus was teaching in the temple courtyard when he was challenged by the chief priests as to what authority he was teaching by. Jesus said he would ask them a question and if they answered him, he would answer them. They did not, so he did not (see Luke 20:1–8). Later that day, as he was leaving the temple, Jesus told his apostles about the coming destruction of the temple and by extension the destruction of the Jewish nation.

The following day, Wednesday, Judas Iscariot, one of the apostles, went to talk with the church leaders. They had previously contacted Judas and let him know they wanted to bring Jesus before the Sanhedrin so they could question him. They agreed that he would turn Jesus over to them at a time and place where no one could thwart his capture. They paid him. Later, he claimed he had no idea they had planned to have him killed.

Thursday was the day of unleavened bread, the day the Passover lamb had to be sacrificed. Jesus instructed his disciples to make preparations to eat the Passover meal in the upper room of Mark's house. Jesus and his disciples reclined at the table to partake of what became known as the Last Supper. Jesus took the cup, blessed it, drank from it, and passed it around. He took the bread, gave thanks, broke it, and gave it to them, saying, "This is my body given for you: do this in remembrance of me." In the same way, after supper, he took the cup, saying, "This cup is the new covenant in my blood, which is poured out for you." (Luke 22:19, 20).

Shortly after Jesus said someone at the table would betray him, Judas Iscariot left the table. In the discussion that followed, Peter stated that he was prepared to go with Jesus to prison or even death. Jesus told him that before the rooster crowed that day, Peter would deny him three times.

They sang a song before going to the Mount of Olives to pray, as was their custom. When they reached the place, Jesus withdrew from them, knelt down, and prayed,

> "Father, if you are willing, take this cup from me; yet
> not my will, but yours be done." An angel from heaven
> appeared to him and strengthened him. And being in
> anguish, he prayed more earnestly, and his sweat was like
> drops of blood falling to the ground. (Luke 22:42–44)

Critics have often said that the claim Jesus actually sweated blood is the product of a vivid imagination and is just another reason to doubt the writers of the gospel. It is now known that under extreme psychological stress, the human body often will release a chemical that may break down the capillaries in the sweat glands and cause the release of small amounts of blood. This condition is called hematidrosis. Though rare, it can and does occur.

After praying, he went back to his disciples. While he was talking to them, a large group of chief priests, armed temple guards, and elders led by Judas appeared. As Judas approached Jesus to kiss him, he asked, "Judas, are you betraying the Son of Man with a kiss?" (Luke 22:48). Jesus was arrested and led away a captive while his disciples scattered into the darkness of night.

### Peter's Denial

They took Jesus into the house of the high priest; Peter followed at a distance. He sat with a group of people. A servant girl implicated him as one of Jesus' followers. Peter strongly denied it. A little later, someone else stated that Peter was indeed one of them. "Man, I am not!" Peter replied. About an hour later, another asserted that as a Galilean, he must be one of them. Peter replied, "Man, I don't know what you're talking about!" Just then the rooster crowed. "The Lord turned and looked straight at Peter" (Matthew 22:61). Peter left and wept bitterly.

## The Trial

Throughout Friday night (after six Thursday evening), Jesus was held captive. The guards blindfolded him, struck him repeatedly, and mocked him. He was brought before the high priest, Caiaphas, who, along with the council known as the Sanhedrin, questioned him and presented two men who testified falsely against Jesus. None brought believable evidence. In exasperation, Caiaphas asked him if he was the Messiah, the Son of God. "You have said so," Jesus replied. "But I say to all of you: From now on you will see the Son of Man sitting at the right hand of the Mighty One and coming on the clouds of heaven" (Matthew 26:64).

That was all Caiaphas needed. He now had his charge, blasphemy. Turning to the Sanhedrin, he asked them what they thought. They answered that he was worthy of death. Since the Sanhedrin did not have the authority to order the death penalty, they bound him and turned him over to one who did, the governor, Pilate.

The governor could find no basis for the death penalty, but he did learn that Jesus was a Galilean. Galilee was under Herod Antipas', son of Herod the Great, jurisdiction, and Herod happened to be in Jerusalem, so Pilate sent him to his new friend, Herod. After hearing Jesus' accusers, Herod ridiculed Jesus, dressed him up in an elegant robe, and finding no cause to continue with the proceedings, sent him back to Pilate.

Pilate, knowing there were no grounds for execution but hearing the cries from Caiaphas, the Sanhedrin, and the crowds around his home demanding his crucifixion, offered to have him flogged instead. Unrelenting, the crowd continued to insist on Jesus' crucifixion. Not wanting to crucify him, Pilate grasped at another opportunity to possibly have him released. During the festival season, it was the governor's custom to release a prisoner chosen by the crowd. He gave them the choice of releasing Jesus or another well-known prisoner, Barabbas. They demanded the release of Barabbas and the crucifixion of Jesus. Pilate literally washed his hands before the crowd and told them Jesus' blood was on their heads. Pilate ordered the soldiers to take Jesus, flog him, and then crucify him. Judas Iscariot, realizing what he had done, hanged himself.

## The Scourging

The whips used by the executioners were designed to inflict maximum pain without killing the prisoner. Hence, Roman custom dictated no more than thirty-nine lashes; they knew most prisoners would not survive forty or more. The whips were made of braided leather with metal balls and sharp bone woven in.

The soldiers took Jesus to a public square, stripped his torso, and tied him to a flogging post. They began the brutal, torturous flogging. Each lash would leave deep contusions in his supersensitive back from the metal balls and lacerations from the sharp bones. With each additional blow, the contusions would deepen and would break open, causing long, bloody gashes. After the last lash, his back, from his shoulders down to his upper legs, was totally brutalized, beaten to a pulp, and bleeding.

The soldiers released him, held him up, and put a purple robe on his beaten body and a crown of thorns on his head. They mocked him, called him king of the Jews, and continued to strike his body and head with a staff. They removed the purple robe, put his own clothes back on him, and led him off to be crucified.

## The Torturous Walk to Golgotha

It was the custom that the person being crucified would be forced to carry the top cross member of his cross to the crucifixion site. Jesus' body was so brutalized that the soldiers had to solicit the help of a bystander, Simon, to help Jesus carry the cross.

When after the long torturous walk they finally reached Golgotha ("the place of the skull") Jesus most certainly would have been experiencing severe hypovolemic shock caused by his severe loss of blood. This condition would have caused his heart to race to replace the blood that wasn't there, his blood pressure would have dropped severely, causing fainting and collapse, his kidneys would have stopped producing urine to conserve bodily fluids, and he would have experienced severe thirst. Of these, the two visible symptoms, collapse and thirst were recorded.

## The Crucifixion and Entombment

At Golgotha, Jesus was laid on the crossbeam, arms outstretched, and six- to seven- inch tapered metal spikes were driven through each wrist. The wrist, in the language of the day, was considered part of the hand. The pain of each spike going through the large nerve in each wrist must have been absolute torture, added on top of the torture Jesus was already experiencing.

He was then raised to attach the horizontal crossmember to the permanent vertical crossmember. He experienced more extreme pain as another large metal spike was driven through his feet. The immediate effect would have been a severe stretching of the arms with complete dislocation of both shoulders from their sockets. "Jesus said, 'Father, forgive them for they do not know what they are doing'" (Luke 23:34).

The time was about nine Friday morning. Having done their job, the soldiers sat down near the cross and cast lots among themselves for Jesus' clothes. From their position, they could plainly read the sign they had nailed over Jesus' head, "This is Jesus, the King of the Jews" (Matthew 27:37). They had nothing to do but wait.

It is now known that death on the cross was usually by slow, very painful asphyxiation. In his weakened and hypovolemic state, with all his weight on his strained and outstretched arms, the muscles in his chest would have put him in a permanently inhaled position. To exhale, he would have had to shift the position of his chest muscles by lifting his body. With the spike through his feet, this process was excruciatingly painful. Every time he lifted his body to exhale, the spike would tear sinew, muscle, and nerve, elongating the hole punctured by the spike through his already heavily bleeding feet. The pain was so severe that only a new word could describe it: *excruciating*—from the cross.

It was noon on Friday. This torturous breathing process labored on, then the skies darkened, bright bolts of lightning streaked across the heavens and lit up the mountainsides, loud claps of thunder echoed across the valley, and a deep, penetrating darkness set in. The tortuous breathing process, even more laborious than before, continued.

### Handing His Mother Over to John

Jesus raised his vision, looked around, and saw his mother and John the apostle standing by the cross. He looked at her and softly whispered, "Woman, here is your son," and to the disciple, "Here is your mother" (John 19:26–27). With those words, Jesus put his beloved mother in the care of his disciple.

It was almost three Friday afternoon. Breathing was almost nonexistent. Jesus said, "I am thirsty" (John 19:28). A soldier put a sponge dipped in wine vinegar on a stalk of a hyssop plant and put it near Jesus' mouth. He received the drink and turned away.

### God Forsakes His Son

A moment later, Jesus' body stiffened, he let out a cry, and in a strained voice, he cried, "Eli, Eli, lema sabachthani?" "My God, My God, why have you forsaken me?" (Matthew 27:46). Racked with excruciating pain, he most certainly knew God had to leave him. Still, when he actually felt God turning his back on him and moving away, it was more than he could silently bear. At that moment, Jesus took the sins of the world unto himself. God, unable to be near sin, turned his back and left him, just as he had to do when he left Adam and put him out of the garden of Eden when sin came to dwell in Adam.

## The Death

Jesus' body relaxed, he accepted the loneliness, and he said, "It is finished" (John 19:30). The darkness deepened, and with his breathing barely perceptible Jesus said in a faltering voice, "Father, into your hands I commit my spirit." When he had said this, he breathed his last (Luke 23:46).

## The New Covenant

Amid peals of thunder and flashes of lightning, the heavy veil separating the worship place from the holy of holies in the temple was ripped top to bottom. This proclaimed to the world that humanity was then under a new covenant. The price for our sins had been paid. We could now access God the Father through his Son. We no longer had to sacrifice for the atonement of our sins. The perfect sacrifice had been made.

## The Injustice

The Roman centurion (a leader of hundreds) who had witnessed the proceedings praised God and said, "Surely this was a righteous man" (Luke 23:47). A man who had undoubtedly seen hundreds of crucifixions, who had led many men in battle, most probably a Gentile, realized that an incredible injustice had just been committed.

### Certifying Death

It was less than three hours until the Jewish Sabbath started. Bodies could not stay on the cross through the Sabbath. To speed up death, the soldiers would break the legs of the crucified so they could not raise their bodies to breathe. This they did to the two who were crucified with Jesus. When they came to Jesus, they saw he was dead, but to make sure, one of the soldiers ran a spear through him. Seeing blood and water rush out, he was satisfied there was no life left in him.

### The Burial

Joseph of Arimathea, a wealthy man, a dissenting member of the Sanhedrin, and a follower of Christ, asked Pilate for the body of Jesus so he could bury him before six that evening, when the Sabbath would start. Pilate, after receiving confirmation of Jesus' death from his professional executioners, agreed to release the body to Joseph. Joseph had Jesus taken down, cleaned, anointed, wrapped in burial linen, and put into a new tomb. They rolled a massive stone that tightly sealed the tomb. All of this was done before the start of the Sabbath. It was approximately four or five o'clock Friday afternoon. Some of the women followers of Jesus who had been with him from Galilee stood at a distance and watched all of this.

### Securing the Tomb

On Saturday, the chief priests and the Pharisees went to Pilate.

> "Sir," they said, "We remember that while he was still alive that deceiver said, 'After three days I will rise again.' So give the order for the tomb to be made secure until the third day. Otherwise, his disciples may come and steal the body and tell the people that he has been raised

from the dead. This last deception will be worse than the first." "Take a guard," Pilate answered. "Go and make the tomb as secure as you know how." So they went and made the tomb secure by putting a seal on the stone and posting the guard. (Matthew 27:63–66)

### Reanointing the Body

On Sunday, the first day of the week, Mary Magdalene (one of the women who had watched and agonized over the complete crucifixion) and two other women were on their way to the tomb at daybreak. They were going to the tomb with spices to anoint the body of Jesus. As they approached the tomb, they wondered who might help them roll the heavy stone sealing the tomb away so they could enter.

As they were on their way, they felt an earthquake. The stone rolled away. The guards, seeing what they thought was an angel, fell to the ground and "became like dead men" (Matthew 28:4).

### The Body Is Gone!

When the women arrived at the tomb, they saw the stone had been rolled away. They entered the tomb and did not find the body of Jesus. Two men in gleaming clothes said to them, "Why do you look for the living among the dead? He is not here; he has risen! Remember how he told you ... 'The Son of Man must be delivered over to the hands of sinners, be crucified and on the third day be raised again.' Then they remembered his words" (Luke 24:5–8). "So the women hurried away from the tomb, afraid yet filled with joy." Jesus appeared to them and said, "Do not be afraid. Go and tell my brothers" (Matthew 27:8, 10).

### Unbelief and Doubt

The women ran back to the disciples and told the eleven apostles all they had seen and heard, "But they did not believe" (Luke 24:11). Peter, though doubtful, ran to the tomb and saw it was empty except for a few strips of linen lying by themselves.

### The Cover Story

> While the women were on their way, some of the guards went into the city and reported to the chief priests everything that had happened. When the chief priests had met with the elders and devised a plan, they gave the soldiers a large sum of money, telling them, "You are to say, 'His disciples came during the night and stole him away while we were asleep.' If this report gets to the governor, we will satisfy him and keep you out of trouble." So the soldiers took the money and did as they were instructed. And this story has been widely circulated among the Jews to this very day. (Matthew 28:11–15)

### On the Road to Emmaus

On the same day, Cleopas and another disciple were going to Emmaus, a village about seven miles from Jerusalem. Jesus came up and walked with them. They talked about scripture, about the death of the prophet, and about the story the women had told them about the empty tomb. They did not recognize who he was until they sat down to eat. When they recognized him, he vanished.

### *Jesus Appears to All the Apostles*

That same day, Sunday, while the two Jesus had joined on the road to Emmaus were excitingly telling the apostles back in Jerusalem about their encounter with the risen Christ,

> Jesus himself stood among them and said to them, "Peace be with you ... Why are you troubled, and why do doubts rise in your minds? Look at my hands and feet. It is I myself! Touch me and see, a ghost does not have flesh and bones, as you see I have. Do you have anything to eat?" They gave him a piece of broiled fish, and he took it and ate it in their presence. (Luke 34:38, 39)

### *Other Appearances*

Jesus walked among them for forty days, teaching them and clarifying all he had said to them before. On one occasion, he appeared before 500 worshippers. In Galilee, he continued to perform miracles with his disciples, and in discussions with Peter, he was in essence forgiven for his denials after Jesus' arrest.

### *The Great Commission and the Ascension*

On the last day, the eleven disciples went to the mountain in Galilee as they had been instructed.

> Then Jesus came to them and said, "All authority in heaven and on earth has been given to me. Therefore go and make disciples of all nations, baptizing them in the name of the Father and of the Son and of the Holy Spirit, and teaching them to obey everything I have commanded you. And surely I am with you always, to the very end of the age." (Matthew 28:18–20)

> After he had said this, he was taken up before their very eyes, and a cloud hid him from their sight. They were looking intently up into the sky as he was going, when suddenly two men dressed in white stood beside them. "Men of Galilee," they said, "why do you stand here looking into the sky? This same Jesus, who has been taken from you into heaven, will come back in the same way you have seen him go into heaven." (Acts 1:9–11)

## Summary

Although I have explained the gospel based on scripture, there are sufficient secular writings that could almost allow us to write the gospel story without referring to scripture: Flavius Josephus: "Jesus was called the Christ." Talmud: "He did 'magic.' He led Israel into new teachings, and was hanged on Passover for them." Tacitus: "in Judea." Eliezar: "but claimed to be God and would return." Pliny the Younger: "which his followers believed, worshipping him as God."

And this is the gospel, the good news—Jesus, being God, coming to earth as a man to feel all that we feel, to be tempted with all that we are tempted by, to feel the grief, the joy, the pain, the love that we feel, and much more than any of us, to suffer insufferable torture and death to remove the insurmountable obstacle between us and God, to take all our sins and wash them away with the blood of his sacrifice. But why? There is only one word that can suffice, that can explain what he feels for us—love.

# Chapter 18

# The Resurrection—Did It Really Happen?

A number of pivotal and critical beliefs are absolutes in Christians' faith. Though they are not great in number, the removal of any one of them would be fatal to their belief. We have seen that proving the Bible is inaccurate or untruthful would certainly be fatal to Christianity. Proving that the resurrection of Jesus is a myth or wishful thinking and did not occur would be another.

In 1 Corinthians 15:14, the apostle Paul agreed on the critical nature of the resurrection and clearly stated, "And if Christ has not been raised, our preaching is useless, and so is your faith." In the same letter to the Corinthians in verse 17, he wrote, "And if the Christ has not been raised, your faith is futile; you are still in your sins." In verse 20, he assured us, "But Christ has indeed been raised from the dead, the first fruits of those who have fallen asleep. For since death came through a man, the resurrection of the dead comes also through a man. For as in Adam all die, so in Christ all will be made alive."

So okay, the Bible says Jesus was resurrected. Is there any other proof of his resurrection? Any evidence outside that which is stated in the Bible that would substantiate the claim? There have in fact been several "trials" that have been held to prove the validity or invalidity of the resurrection. These "trials" used the same standards of evidence and proof that regular U.S. courts would accept. We will take a look at some of the evidence, objective and circumstantial, that would be considered adequate and substantive proof in a courtroom.

# The Empty Tomb

## *Did Jesus Really Die?*

Let's address an oft-heard question: Did Jesus really die? Perhaps he only fainted and after he was lowered from the cross and while being prepared for burial, he woke up. Remember that between six and nine that Friday morning, Jesus had been severely lashed with whips designed to rip and tear open the flesh, had been continually beaten by Roman soldiers, forced to carry the cross at least part of the way to Golgotha, and was nailed to the cross. By that time, he had already suffered severe blood loss.

He then started to bleed from the spike wounds in his wrists and the larger spike through his feet. He was laboring to gasp for air while hanging from outstretched arms and dislocated shoulders. This struggle went on for six hours until, not being able to breathe, he died. A little later, a soldier, trying to make sure he was dead, ran him through with a spear, and blood and water gushed out.

Any one of the three traumas—severe blood loss, asphyxiation, being lanced—could have killed him. To believe he could have survived all three exceeds credulity. Pilate's executioner (certainly not a novice at painfully killing people) attested to his death. We must also remember that for Roman soldiers, the penalty for failure to carry out their duty of execution would have been death. Yes, Jesus did die.

## *Do We Know Where He Was Buried?*

Where he was buried was no secret. There were several witnesses to the location of the tomb and as many witnesses to the placement of the body of Jesus in the tomb and its sealing and securing. Were there guards securing the tomb? Yes, the chief priests, to make sure the body was not stolen, would have ensured that the tomb was securely guarded. They surely would not have guarded just any tomb; they would have been sure to guard the correct tomb.

## Did Women Really Discover the Empty Tomb?

The discovery of the empty tomb on the Sunday morning by three women is noteworthy. In the culture of the time, women certainly had lower status than men. The judicial system of the day disallowed the testimony of women. You had to be a man to be considered worthy of truthful and factual testimony. But the authors of the Gospels each recorded that women had made this momentous discovery.

There is no doubt; if this were a myth, the discovery would have been made by a person or persons with stature—perhaps a priest, a Roman centurion, or some other important personage. No, the fact that the discovery was made by women and not altered—as would have been the temptation to elevate the credibility of the discovery—attests to its authenticity.

## Was the Body Stolen?

Why was the tomb empty when the women approached? Had Jesus' followers stolen the body during the night and hid it so they could start a new religion based on his resurrection? We will see that the chief priests essentially claimed the body had been stolen. But there are several reasons that the stealing of the body was not a plausible reason for the empty tomb.

1. The tomb was guarded around the clock by Roman soldiers.
2. The tomb had been sealed by a heavy boulder.
3. The guards would have had to have been overpowered, but there was never any mention of this by the chief priests or the guards themselves.

4. Some of the burial garments were left in the tomb, inconsistent with the movement of a body for reburial.

5. The implausible story concocted by the chief priests and passed on by the Jews to this day that the body was stolen by his followers after the guards fell asleep is not believable because the penalty for guards' sleeping at their posts was death, and if they were asleep, how could they have known that it was Jesus' followers who stole the body?

6. The most compelling reason that the body was not stolen is provided by the actual fate of the apostles. I will discuss this in more detail in the section on the "Apostles" below, as the discussion unfolds.

### Was the Tomb Really Empty?

Skeptics often question why so much time is spent on trying to explain why the tomb was empty. What proof is there that the tomb was in fact empty? At first, this appears to be an excellent question, but upon examination, it is soon evident that the opposite is true.

The chief priests needed something, anything, to disprove that Jesus was the Messiah and that his claims of resurrection within three days were baseless. What better proof could they have than merely to unlock the tomb and exhibit the lifeless body of Jesus? This they could not do because there was no body to exhibit. No, the tomb was empty.

## The Witnesses

### Did Anybody See Him after His "Resurrection"?

Having established that the tomb was empty, did anybody see him on earth, or did he just come back to life and go straight to heaven? No, Jesus was seen the very day he resurrected by the women who discovered the empty tomb, by the apostles Peter and John, by two disciples on their way to Emmaus, and by all the remaining apostles that evening. Jesus appeared to the apostles in the room where they had been hiding since the crucifixion.

Most biblical scholars would state that they were not only hiding, they were in fact cowering, afraid for their lives since the moment they ran from and abandoned their Christ to the soldiers and the chief priests.

## Could He Have Just Been a Ghost?

Christ appeared, and after reassuring them that it was he in the flesh, he allowed them to touch him, question him, and then he ate with them. After the resurrection, Christ was on earth forty days and appeared to many others.

The apostle Paul in 1 Corinthians 15:6–8 stated that after appearing to the apostles,

> he appeared to more than five hundred of the brothers and sisters at the same time, most of whom are still living, though some have fallen asleep. Then he appeared to James, then to all the apostles, and last of all he appeared to me also.

## Perhaps Paul Just Wanted to Believe

Paul's testimony is very credible. Evidence shows that he first made this statement to the Corinthians within twenty-five years after the resurrection. Most of the people Christ appeared to were still alive, though a few had died (fallen asleep). The chief priests and other detractors would have loved to have gotten their hands on some of these witnesses and had them publicly deny the resurrection, but there is not one record of or mention of any witness disavowing the resurrection.

So we have five to six hundred eyewitnesses to the resurrected Christ. Most of them would have been alive when some of the Gospels were written and used to preach the resurrection. Certainly, many were still alive when Paul spread the resurrection story and when he wrote some of his epistles, or letters, confirming the resurrection. Yet none contradicted the story as it was told and written. It is difficult to have more objective evidence to support the resurrection of the Christ. Yes, he was resurrected.

## Jesus' Family

### *Did Jesus Appear to His Family?*

I will draw your attention to another statement of Paul in the reference above from 1 Corinthians: "Then he appeared to James." There were two apostles named James, but he already said he had appeared to the apostles, so this James was not one of the apostles. The Bible points out in the Gospels that Jesus had four brothers—James, Cephas (Peter), Jude, and John. He also had some sisters, but they are not named.

### *Out of His Mind*

In Mark 2 and 3, Jesus had been preaching, healing the sick and crippled, being followed and crowded by throngs of people, saying he was the Lord of the Sabbath, and claiming he had divine authority. In a somewhat startling turn of events, Mark 3:21 tells us, "When his family heard about this, they went to take charge of him, for they said, 'He is out of his mind.'" Certainly, prior to the resurrection, Jesus' family members could not be considered followers; they doubted his mental stability! So the resurrected Christ indeed had a very clear reason for visiting his brother James. You can only imagine James's reaction. His mother would have told him his brother had paid the ultimate price for his claims, the very claims she and the rest of the family had thought were crazy!

The Bible tells us that Jesus' brother James played a very key role in the leadership of the early Christian church. Additionally, James and Jude each wrote a book included in the New Testament. Jesus' postresurrection appearance to James certainly turned his family around! They became ardent followers of Christ.

## The Apostles

Jesus' family went from calling him mentally unstable to being his ardent followers. What about the apostles? We saw them abandoning Jesus and scurrying into the night. Rather than anxiously awaiting the promised resurrection, we next saw them meekly cowering in their room, bemoaning the loss of their leader, and wondering what they were going to do next. But when Jesus was resurrected, he appeared to them and others, gave them specific instructions, and ascended into heaven.

### *Could an Illusion Explain the Resurrection Story?*

Having been provided with the preponderance of evidence in favor of the resurrection and appearances of Christ, some critics have stated that an illusion could explain the whole resurrection, that he really did not appear but just *appeared* to have appeared.

There was indeed a time when this illusion theory was given some credence—not much, but some. Illusions are created by the external introduction of hallucinatory chemicals or an internal imbalance of certain chemicals normally caused by severe depravation. The only way it could be done on a large scale would be in a controlled environment, such as the Nazi concentration camps or Woodstock.

Even then, the hallucinations would be individual visions; not everyone would see or imagine the same thing. These circumstances are beyond the realm of probability; one or two isolated cases possibly, but hundreds at one time and for an extended period? No. This was not an illusion.

### How Did the Apostles React to the Resurrection?

After Jesus ascended, did the apostles go back into their room and cower? Were they afraid for their lives? Were they worried about what they were going to do next? The answer to all of these questions is no.

### The First Major Conversion

Just a few days after the ascension, Peter preached to a large crowd in Jerusalem, in the temple courtyard known as Solomon's Colonnade. That day, three thousand became followers of Christ. A few days later, over two thousand were converted. The chief priests and elders of the old establishment must have thought, *Here we go again!* But this time, they were going to nip it in the bud, so to speak.

### The Established Church's Reaction

The apostles Peter and John were arrested and brought before the Sanhedrin and the high priest. They were severely chastised, and under severe threats, they were admonished and commanded "not to speak or teach at all in the name of Jesus. But Peter and John replied, 'Which is right in God's eyes: to listen to you, or to him? You be the judges! As for us, we cannot help speaking about what we have seen and heard'" (Acts 4:18–20).

## Initial Growth of Christianity

So much for timidity and cowering before the authorities! From the resurrection on, the apostles spoke with authority, healed the sick and lame, and converted many to the way of the Lord. They did not deviate from the ministry of Jesus; they preached it with great assurance and conviction. They were beginning to be perceived as real threats to the established religion and government.

## The Martyrdom of the Apostles

This threat was so real to the authorities that one by one, the apostles were martyred. The apostle James was the first to be beheaded not long after the beginning of the church. Years later, the apostle Peter was crucified; tradition has it that at his request, he was crucified upside down because he did not consider himself worthy to die like Jesus.

## The Last Witness

All the apostles were martyred except John, whose brother James had been the first apostle martyred. Church tradition has John being boiled in oil late in his ministry but surviving without even the smell of smoke on his body. He was imprisoned on the island of Patmos. While there, he had a vision and was told to write the apocalyptic book we now call Revelation. John died a natural death in his late nineties.

## The Ultimate Proof

All but one of the apostles were persecuted and martyred for the ministry, yet none denied his belief in Jesus. What was the one factor that changed them from timid, cowering individuals to people willing to die and actually dying for their beliefs? It wasn't their knowledge of Jesus and his ministry; they had been with him, they had known him, and they had participated in his ministry. No, it was something bigger than that: they had seen him die, they knew he had been buried, and they had seen him alive. The resurrection gave them all the proof they needed. They knew he was God, and they knew his message was true, so nothing else mattered; everything else was secondary.

### Haven't Others Died For Their Beliefs?

Most skeptics will agree that dying for your beliefs is something special. However, that alone will not prove Christianity is the one true religion. People of many major religions have been known to die for their beliefs; extreme Muslims willingly martyr themselves for what they believe in. Although this does appear to be a good point, there is however a very significant difference. History has shown that people sometimes have (and still do) die for a religion they believe is true. However, it is something quite different to believe that people would willingly die for a belief they knew was false.

If the apostles had stolen the body of Jesus from the tomb, as the high priests asserted, they would have known that Jesus had not resurrected and their belief would have been false. If the apostles had not witnessed the resurrection, based on their previous cowering before authorities, it is very unlikely that they would have had the courage or conviction for martyrdom. No, the apostles not only believed that their faith was real and true, they knew it. They had been witnesses; they had seen the proof! And they were willing to die for what they knew was a true belief.

## The Church

To this point, we have a lone carpenter who was crucified, his twelve followers reduced to eleven because one had betrayed him, a few loyal women supporters, and a somewhat less-than-enthusiastic core of followers in and around Jerusalem.

We have also seen that the resurrection turned everything around. The apostles, energized and enthused, converted many followers. This enthusiasm and apparent disregard for the authority of the established church quickly brought them under the severe scrutiny of the chief priests and elders of the temple so much so that they began a serious campaign of persecution against the new believers.

### Saul of Tarsus

Among these persecutors was the chief persecutor of them all, Saul of Tarsus. He was about twenty-five when he made his appearance in the Bible. He was born in Cilicia, making him a natural-born citizen of Rome. He was educated and trained by one of the most prestigious teachers in Jerusalem, Gamaliel. He was thoroughly versed in the scriptures and was a Pharisee in good standing in the established church. He was indeed an up-and-coming young man.

Saul's main preoccupation, without doubt very sincere and very zealous, was to save his church from these interlopers with their false and heretical beliefs. One of these believers arrested and brought before the Sanhedrin for trial was Stephen.

### The Martyrdom of Stephen

The disciple (student) Stephen, who almost assuredly listened to Jesus preach and probably walked with him, was a very knowledgeable and ardent speaker. After he presented an inscrutable defense based on scripture, the very annoyed elders were furious and gnashed their teeth, knowing they had been severely chastised using their own scriptures.

Stephen, being completely comfortable in his faith in the risen Christ, "looked up to heaven and saw the glory of God, and Jesus standing at the right hand of God. 'Look he said, I see heaven open and the Son of Man standing at the right hand of God'" (Acts 7:55–56).

This was more than they could bear! They had him dragged out of the city and started stoning him! "While they were stoning him, Stephen prayed, 'Lord Jesus, receive my spirit.' Then he fell on his knees and cried out, 'Lord do not hold this sin against them.' When he had said this, he fell asleep" (Acts 7:59–60). Thus the spirit of the first postresurrection martyr recorded in the New Testament was received into heaven. Supervising the stoning was the chief persecutor, Saul of Tarsus.

### Dispersal of the Believers

After the martyrdom of Stephen and the relentless persecution of Christ's followers, a mass exodus of believers from Jerusalem occurred. Biblical scholars attribute a significant part of the explosive growth of Christianity in such a short time to this dispersal of believers throughout the country and into other countries. Though they left Jerusalem, they did not lose their ardor or their belief and continued to spread the word.

### Saul Becomes Paul

Another significant factor in this growth was the chief persecutor, Saul. On one of his trips to Damascus (yes, the very one in the news today, Damascus in Syria) to round up more heretics, he had an incident. Jesus appeared to him! Saul's conversion was sudden and complete. He became just as ardent a follower of Christ as he had been a persecutor of Christ's followers. His special commission was to minister to and convert the Gentiles.

This he did fervently and successfully. The Bible records his three long and fruitful missions throughout Asia and what is now Turkey, Greece, and Italy. He had plans to go to Spain, but if he did go, the Bible does not record it. In addition to his missions, Paul (yes, Jesus changed his name also) is known to have written thirteen of the twenty-seven New Testament books, and there is evidence that he also wrote the book of Hebrews; if so, that would be his fourteenth. Through his New Testament books, Paul had not stopped preaching the Word he died for; he was martyred by Nero in AD 67/68 at age sixty-three.

### The Apostles and Continued Growth

The apostles stayed in Jerusalem for the most part. In between arrests, persecution, and being jailed, they actively grew the church. As the small membership continued to grow, they met in each other's homes, they shared their belongings, and they continued to break bread together as Jesus had done with them.

Within twenty years of the crucifixion and resurrection, the small group of people that had been his followers grew into a church that had believers in the very court of Caesar's palace in Rome!

## Summary

At the start of this chapter on the resurrection, I started by saying that there were a few but very critical pivotal matters in Christendom. One was the trustworthiness and truthfulness of the Bible, and another was the resurrection of Jesus. If either were proven false, Christianity could not exist, at least not in the manner and intent that God had established. Unfortunately, there are many pretenders in the world today claiming to be Christians while disavowing major segments of the Bible and often stating that Jesus is not or may not be the Messiah, thus rejecting the deity of Christ. By the admission of their beliefs, they reject the basis for Christianity!

But getting back to the resurrection—we have more than enough evidence to prove the historicity in any American court not only of Jesus himself but also of his resurrection. This evidence includes

1. The empty tomb: Jesus was buried, the tomb was sealed, guards secured the tomb, his followers did not steal the body, and the chief priests could not produce the body of Jesus. The body was not in the tomb!

2. The witnesses: The witnesses were plentiful. At a minimum, there were over five hundred and twenty-five eyewitnesses, and at least five of these eyewitnesses wrote about their encounter with the risen Christ. They did not write about their encounters and stash them away in a safe place somewhere. No, they distributed their written records around for the world to see. Many of those who saw the writings would have been witnesses themselves, so any untruths would have been immediately made public. Nobody ever challenged the writings.

3. Jesus' family: At one time, they thought he was crazy. After James saw his resurrected brother, they became ardent followers. If his family were skeptics, how about Paul of Tarsus? No doubt he was a skeptic until that encounter with Jesus on one of his persecution trips. That is pretty convincing proof of one major happening!

4. The apostles: There is no better proof of the resurrection than the complete turnaround of the apostles. From cowering, to complete acceptance, to actually going to their executions proclaiming the truth of their resurrected Lord—evidentiary proof gets no better than that.

5. The church: The church saw such spectacular growth that something exceedingly extraordinary must have occurred to elicit such faith, belief, tenacity, and sacrifice from its followers. The sacrifice was indeed great because in the years up to about AD 300, thousands upon thousands of Christ's followers were martyred in many ways. The resurrected Christ is the only viable explanation. Of special note is the fact that Christianity is a volitional religion; you become a Christian by exercising your free will and understanding. You cannot say the same for the second-largest religion, Islam.

Any one of the above could conceivably be argued as insufficient proof of the resurrection. However, when you take them all together, they can and do provide insurmountable proof. Anyone who wants more proof will forever deny the truth. Scripture acknowledges there are those who regardless of the proof will continue to deny; they are those who will harden their hearts and not accept the truth.

## The Survivability of Christianity

When this carpenter started his ministry, he had nothing and was nothing in the eyes of the world, which Rome ruled. The established church and the emperors of Rome did everything in their power to remove him from the scene, to eradicate his religion, and to ensure their own religion would prevail. In less than forty years after his crucifixion, the temple of the established church had been totally destroyed, and a few years later, the established church itself was disbursed to the four corners of the world. Some 425 years after the resurrection, Rome itself would cease to be an empire.

### *The Carpenter and His Church*

And the religion started by the carpenter? It lived on to be the largest religion in the world, and it so remains to this very day. This one carpenter from the small village of Nazareth impacted the world in a way that had never been experienced before and never will again—until the *parousia*, his Second Coming.

# Chapter 19

# The Christian Life

## The Foundation of the Church

We have seen with more than sufficient evidence that Christianity has very strong underpinnings, a solid foundation. A very large portion of Christianity was developed in plain view of a number of eyewitnesses. On the other hand, many other religions started with "revelations" received by a single person, e.g., Mormonism, Buddhism, and Islam.

Secular evidence of Christianity's establishment, growth, and beliefs abound in the archaeological and historical records, with abundant historical support for its early stages of development provided by the Old Testament. The New Testament provides guidance for the continued growth and maturation of Christianity.

### Christianity and Other Religions

Christianity has many characteristics that distinguish it from other major religions. The most significant is that it is the only religion whose founder was tortured, crucified, died, buried, and resurrected. He was not revived, he was not resuscitated—he was resurrected. He came back to life from the dead! Scripture shows that in his ministry, Jesus miraculously brought several people back to life after they had died. Every one of these people, however, did later die. Joseph Smith, the founder or Mormonism, died. Siddhartha Guatama, who later became known simply as the Buddha, died. Muhammad, who founded Islam, died. None of their followers even claimed their spiritual leaders came back to life.

Only Jesus came back to life, never to taste death again! In this part of the discussion, most skeptics would be very conflicted because acceptance of this concept is beyond their comprehension. They cannot accept it! Perhaps reviewing the evidentiary proof provided in the previous chapter might help. Remember that the will must cooperate with the mind or forever remain conflicted.

Another major distinctive characteristic of Christianity is the way a Christian is assured of eternal life. Buddhism does not address the afterlife. Mormons and Muslims seek to attain eternal life primarily by what they do, while Christians receive eternal life by what they believe.

Within the present Christian community, there are some differences in interpretation in the believing-only doctrine. Another needed clarification is, when we read the words *save, saved,* or *salvation,* many of us have been conditioned to interpret them as the receiving of eternal life. Biblical studies have shown that over 70 percent of the time these three words are used in the Bible, they are referring to relief from an immediate or imminent danger or threat while in this life. Context is important. Additionally, eternal life refers to being with God for eternity. Death or eternal damnation normally will mean being separated from God and being in hell forever. Again, context.

I must address another important distinction between Christianity and some of the other major religions, the manner in which new converts are made. To grow their number of converts, some religions resort to coercion, threats, and even force. To be a Christian is to have a personal relationship with God. You cannot be coerced into having this relationship; it must be with complete and total free will and understanding on your part.

### *Misuse of the Christian Banner*

I would be remiss if I didn't mention that in the past, more than a few "church" leaders have misused their authority and position to coerce others into agreeing with church doctrine and rules under the banner of Christianity. This coercion sometimes required followers to take actions not sanctioned by the Bible.

The Dark Ages and the Inquisition come to mind. The long and brutal Crusades were another dark period, as was the concept of forced slavery. We don't know if these leaders were sincere in their misguided use of Christianity or if they knowingly and unscrupulously used the banner to further personal goals; only God knows. History shows us that this misuse definitely happened in the past. Our life experiences show us that it is still happening with a disturbing and increasing frequency.

Having said that, it is even more important to note that because the receiver of the message might misuse the message, this does not make the message any less meaningful, useful, or effective when received with an open heart.

## The Christian

So what does a Christian believe? What is a Christian? Quantifying religious beliefs is a difficult proposition. Many have tried to delineate the central Christian beliefs, aka doctrines. I stress *central* because there are over ten thousand denominations, many of which claim the Bible as their own. Practically all of them have written doctrines or at least have written sets of beliefs and rules. So the only thing we can do is go to the Bible.

Several Christian apologetic groups have studied this area extensively. Some of these studies date back to the beginning of the twentieth century, and most have compiled a biblical set of beliefs that are directive in nature. These beliefs are not optional. Using the Bible as the source, it is remarkable how consistent these lists are. In reviewing each one and cross referencing each belief to the Bible, seven have made themselves totally dominant. Each one has a very emphatic biblical tie. Each one has references throughout both testaments. All are very definitive throughout the Bible, and a few have more emphasis in the New Testament. Christian churches have for the most part incorporated all these basic doctrines into their worship procedures. It is clear that the Bible Christian will believe

1. that there is only one true God, the God of the Old and the New Testaments. "I am the first and I am the last; apart from me there is no God" (Isaiah 44:6).
2. that God is a Trinity. God is expressed in three distinct persons: God the Father, God the Son, and God the Holy Spirit. "In the name of the Father and of the Son and of the Holy Spirit" (Matthew 28:9).
3. in the deity of Jesus. Jesus incarnated was fully God and fully man. "Every spirit that acknowledges that Jesus Christ has come in the flesh is from God, but every spirit that does not acknowledge Jesus is not from God" (1 John 4:2–3).
4. in the Gospel. Jesus became flesh, preached a ministry of service and love, was arrested, tried, lashed, crucified, died, buried, and resurrected. He made earthly appearances and ascended into heaven. In what became the earliest Christian creed, the apostle Paul told us, "Christ died for our sins … that he was buried, that he was raised on the third day … that he appeared" (1Corinthians 15:3, 4).
5. that Jesus was resurrected in the body, not as a spirit. When he emerged from the tomb, he was in his physical, immortal body. When he appeared to his disciples, he said, "Look at my hands and my feet. It is I myself! Touch me and see, a ghost does not have flesh and bones, as you see I have" (Luke 24:39).
6. that believing in Jesus Christ by faith will be rewarded with eternal life by the grace of God. It cannot be explained any

better than John the apostle's declaration, "For God so loved the world that he gave his only Son, that whoever believes in him shall not perish but have eternal life" (John 3:16). Then the apostle Paul emphatically said that we cannot do any works to save ourselves. "For it is by grace you have been saved, through faith ... not by works" (Ephesians 2:8, 9). With an even greater emphasis, Paul stated, "If righteousness could be gained through the law [works], Christ died for nothing!" (Galatians 2:21).

7. the only way to God is through Jesus. This concept has oft been called by the postmodernists and other secularists the "scandalous exclusivity of Christianity." The apostle John again explained this to us in his gospel in which Jesus said, "I am the way the truth and the life. No one gets to the Father except through me" (John 14:6). Crystal clear; it leaves no room for equivocation.

### Interpretation of the Bible

The beliefs above certainly are the essentials of Christianity. The Bible is an expansive set of books that, in the aggregate, cover all life. It would be presumptuous to believe that everybody would interpret each and every concept in the Bible exactly the same.

Do we possess the ability to understand the Bible? Many concepts in the Bible provide us with just enough information to give us an idea of what those concepts are, what they mean, or what they are like. Several times in the Bible, Jesus said that we do not have the capacity to understand all that he was telling us. One of these is heaven and hell. What are they really like? We are given enough information to clearly tell us that one is very pleasant while the other is not a place you want to be, especially for all eternity.

Yet as expansive as the Bible is, we are given the ability, with the help of the Holy Spirit, to have sufficient understanding of it to clearly follow in the footsteps of Jesus. We are told, "All Scripture is God-breathed [inspired] and is useful for teaching, rebuking, correcting and training in righteousness, so that the servant of God may be thoroughly equipped for every good work" (2 Timothy 3:16, 17).

## Core Beliefs and Peripherals

St Augustine, one of the founding church fathers, put it very well: "In the essentials, unanimity; in the peripherals, charity." Charity in this context would mean to be forgiving and understanding of people who believe in the core essentials but may not agree with our interpretation of the peripherals. Charity also means we should not be offended or judgmental of their peripheral beliefs and to accept their position as their own. As long as they are adhering to the essentials, we should respect them as the Christians they are. Having determined what the essentials are, we can then establish what a Christian must believe, in accordance with the Bible.

It is helpful to note that of the great number of different Christian denominations in the world, most adhere to the above essentials remarkably well. Most of the differences come in what most would consider the peripherals. With the understanding that many of these denominations would consider that the peripheral they believe in is in fact an "essential," we will move on. Many of the peripherals are a natural extension of one of the essentials. For example one of the peripherals in this discussion would be the virgin birth. The essential, the deity of Christ, would require that Jesus be sinless, and he could be sinless only if he was born of a virgin and not from the seed of man, which carried the sin nature propagated by Adam.

As to the peripherals, make no mistake; they are very important and certainly determine the type of person you are, but they are not the determining factor of whether you are a Christian.

The studies referenced above give the peripherals different names and designations, but a sampling of theses peripherals in addition to the virgin birth include the inerrancy of the Bible, the necessity of baptism for salvation, election, predestination, frequency of communion, musical instruments in the church, child or adult baptism, Saturday or Sunday worship, specific end time interpretations, and many, many others.

### On Being Judgmental

Here is a final thought on the subject of what a Christian believes. The information presented is to provide you with an understanding of what a Christian is in accordance with the Bible; it is not meant to be used to judge others. We cannot see what is in a person's heart; only God can do that, and only he can judge whether someone is a Christian. We cannot and should not.

### How Do I Become a Christian?

We have spent a lot of time and effort in getting to this point. Our efforts thus far have been spent on showing and proving that the Bible is valid and trustworthy; that Jesus was a historical person; that he was crucified, died, was buried, and resurrected; and that Christianity is the one true and valid religion.

### Faith and the Christian Life

We now believe that Jesus was; we arrived at this conclusion intellectually. Now it is up to us to take the next step and enter the experiential phase. The only way to enter this phase is intentionally, of our free will though we have received a lot of proof that has led us to this conclusion intellectually that Jesus was. We cannot achieve eternal life through our intellect (notwithstanding what the Gnostics believe; remember, they believed that knowledge provided the key to eternal life, and they controlled that knowledge).

We must take that final step by faith. We must *believe* in Jesus. If you are uncertain what it means to believe in Jesus, the seven core essentials delineated earlier will help you. The moment we believe in Jesus, everything changes. Different people feel different things, but some feel nothing; they just have a sense something is different.


### What Changes?

Many things *are* different. Though people may not have felt all these things the moment they became believers and though they may not even have been aware they occurred, the Bible states that certain things did occur. At the moment of believing, the person was

1. *Repentant.* Consciously or not, by the act of believing, people's perspective on how they think and how they act and live their lives changes. This is perhaps imperceptible at first, but it does happen.
2. *Justified.* By believing, people are justified and have met the legal requirements of the law. They have accepted Jesus' substitutionary sacrificial atonement (he paid the price) for their sins. Though at this point they are still not righteous, they are immediately clothed with the righteousness of Jesus and are thus acceptable to God, and they may, if need be, enter God's presence.
3. *Regenerate* (born again). Believers are no longer bound to sin but receive and are indwelt by the Holy Spirit, who will guide them and help them discern the things that come from God. With the help of the Holy Spirit, believers are better able to judge between right and wrong.

4. *Sanctified.* Believers are set aside for Christ; they become Christians. The process does not end here, though; the sanctification process is just beginning. This process is not done to them; rather, it is done by them. They are now charged to become more like Christ. They now want to do good things and want to worship and know more about Jesus (reading the Bible frequently and prayerfully is indispensable for obtaining this knowledge). They want to proclaim their belief to others by being baptized and participating in communion. They want to help others and bring them to Christ; in short, they want to be like him. As they progress with their sanctification, they in fact will get closer to Christ. As you can see, the "works" according to scripture come after they believe and have received eternal life. It is the process by which they get closer to God and improve their standing in the kingdom of God.

5. At the Second Coming of Christ, believers will be *glorified.* When they are glorified, they receive a new, immortal, and imperishable body and will no longer know suffering or pain. Glorification and the rewards judgment are the final steps to entering eternity.

## What Is the Effect?

Believers have entered the family of God. Though Christians, they are still in the flesh, and though no longer slaves to sin, they still possess the sin nature and will from time to time fall to temptation. They must ask God for forgiveness and ask for increased strength to resist temptation. If the petition is sincere, God will answer and forgive them.

### What about Sin?

Christians are not immune to sin. The problem arises when "Christians" sin, and are not disturbed by the sin, and go on to sin with increased impunity and with diminishing remorse, if any. And if there is no request for forgiveness or the petition is not sincere, more than likely, they did not *really* believe.

Perhaps they professed belief to satisfy the concerns of someone they respected, or perhaps they were afraid of the consequences and "believed" solely to escape hell (sometimes referred to as merely trying to obtain fire insurance). We could go on with countless scenarios, but the bottom line could be that such "believers" were really pretenders. Above all, believers must believe in Jesus.

### What Is Sin?

Sin is anything not pleasing to God. Scripture says that there is no such thing as a small sin or a big sin; there is sin period. Jesus' brother James said, "For whoever keeps the whole law and yet stumbles at just one point is guilty of breaking all of it" (James 2:10). How do you know when or if you have sinned?

As a Christian, the Holy Spirit within you will point sin out to you, often rather emphatically! The commandments are also there to help you identify sin. However, if you live by the highest commandment of all, love the Lord your God with all you heart, with all your soul, with all your strength, and with all your mind and love your neighbor as yourself, everything will fall into place.

Can Christians really comply with this commandment? No. But they should certainly try. The apostle Paul, in referring to this, the greatest commandment, tells us that love overcomes all sin.

## How Can I Be Sure I Have Eternal Life?

Some rather predominant denominations do not believe that you can ever be sure you have eternal life until judgment day. The apostle Peter wrote,

> Therefore my brothers and sisters, make every effort to confirm your calling and election. For if you do these things, you will never stumble, and you will receive a rich welcome into the eternal kingdom of our Lord and Savior Jesus Christ. (2 Peter 1: 10–11).

He was clearly admonishing us that if we are concerned about our salvation, we are likely to have wasted effort and time in stumbling and wondering about our own final destination. We are to confirm our destination and get on with the work of God.

The apostle John emphasized this point: "Very truly I tell you, whoever hears my word and believes him who sent me has eternal life and will not be judged but has crossed over from death to life" (John 5: 24). He did not say he *may* cross over, nor did he say that by doing the right thing and with a little luck he *might* cross over. No. He said he *has* crossed over. If you need clarification on that, then you don't *want* to believe.

### Can I Lose My Eternal Life?

Once you have believed in Jesus, you cannot lose your salvation. The apostle Paul wrote, "that he who began a good work in you will carry it on to completion until the day of Christ Jesus" (Philippians 1:6).

Jesus said, "Very truly I tell you, whoever hears my word and believes him who sent me has eternal life" (John 5:24).

The apostle John wrote in possibly the most quoted verse of scripture, "that whosoever believes in him shall not perish but have everlasting life" (John 3:16).

Paul later in Timothy proclaimed, "I know whom I have believed and am convinced that he is able to guard what I have entrusted to him until that day" (2 Timothy 1:12).

John concluded his first letter by penning, "I write these things to you who believe in the name of the Son of God so that you may know that you have eternal life" (1 John 5:13). Finally Paul explained, "God makes us stand firm in Christ. He anointed us, set his seal of ownership on us, and put his Spirit in our hearts as a deposit, guaranteeing what is to come" (2 Corinthians 1:21). This assurance, of course, does not extend to pretenders.

I find that visualizing a concept puts it in a clearer perspective.

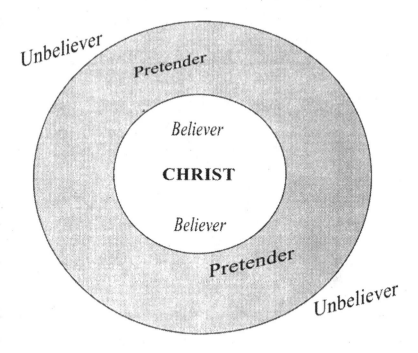

## Circle of Salvation

In the circle of salvation, Christ is at the center of the inner circle while unbelievers are outside the shaded circle. When you believe in Christ through faith, you enter the inner circle and

1. become a member of the family of Christ,
2. establish a relationship with Christ,
3. are assured of eternal life,
4. want to know more about Christ,
5. want to read God's Word,
6. want to do good works, and
7. want to get closer to Christ.

This is a part of your sanctification process. Doing these good works because somebody else says you should or because you want to go to heaven will be of no avail to you. You do them because you want to; this is an expression of your desire to want to know more about Christ and to be more like him. When you sin, as you will (as long as you are in this worldly body), Christ moves away from you. However, he does not expel you from the inner circle. When you repent and ask for forgiveness, he will forgive you, and you can again continue your progress toward Christ. Although the sin is forgiven, the sinner will bear the consequences of that sin.

Those who think or say they believed (superficially, not from the heart) will enter the shaded pretenders circle. They do not have a relationship with Christ. They may attend church, they may even be in the choir, they may continually do good works, but they are not members of Christ's family. They can and often do bounce in and out of the pretenders' circle. Most probably, these are the ones to whom Jesus will say on that day, "I never knew you. Away from me, you evildoers" (Matthew 7:23). If these pretenders ever believe in Christ from the heart, Christ will rejoice and accept them into his inner circle.

A significant number of Christian adherents are told and believe that it is not only possible for them to lose salvation, but also, in many cases, that they have to continually work at it to keep it. In all cases, it is always imperative that the Bible guide us!

### And the Judgment?

As to judgment day, the apostle John in the verse quoted above also made a monumental and most edifying point when he quoted Jesus: "Very truly I tell you, whoever hears my word and believes him who sent me has eternal life and will not be judged but has crossed over from death to life."

With the aid of the Holy Spirit, I can see no other interpretation but that if we believe, we have eternal life, and since we have eternal life, we have already crossed over from death [eternal damnation] to [eternal] life, and therefore there will be no judgment to determine our destination. It is already known!

### Can This Be Confirmed?

I always find referencing the Bible when I have concerns or need explanations to be very helpful. In the matters of salvation and assurance, you will remember that in Matthew 13, Jesus gave us the parable of the sower. You do not want to be any of the first three poor soils that were unreceptive to the seed [His Word]; you want to be the fertile soil that received and grew the seed into a bountiful harvest. That person was the one who heard the Word, believed it, and understood it. A believer.

Having believed, how can we confirm that belief? How can we be sure we are not just deluding ourselves? There are many ways we will know; we will experience a satisfying peace. Things that used to really disturb us may still bring some disturbance, but we will feel they're not nearly as important as they used to be.

You will have a desire and need to read the Word of God. As you read, it will now start to make more sense. After you have spent some time reading it, you will feel a sense of fulfillment. Most importantly, you will begin to feel a love for God. Unbelievers cannot love God because they believe God does not exist or is a fraud, and they cannot love someone who does not exist or is a deceiver.

You will also unconsciously begin to automatically thank him for what you have, for what you experience, and as you mature in the faith, even for some of the trials he sends your way to sharpen your skills, perseverance, and faith.

### *What about Things Out of My Control?*

Major world problems may still raise huge red flags and may be catastrophic, but now you will measure them against a different backdrop. You will understand that most major world upheavals—past, present, and future—have been and will continue to be a manifestation of humanity's proclivity to establish superiority. Most importantly, you will also now know the outcome. Because of that, you will have an inner peace and be thankful.

There are countless other markers that could be used to confirm your belief, but as you mature in the faith, you will no longer feel you need them. As your relationship with God matures, you will just *know*.

## What Happens When I Die?

*It is the destiny of each man to die once, and then the judgment,* Hebrews 9:27.

In this life, one of the most amazing things about being a Christian is that the sting of death disappears! The resurrection of Jesus, being the first to rise in his immortal and glorified body, showed us what was in store for us at his Second Coming. This revelation completely obliterated the sting of death. Having the assurance of eternal life means that dying in this world is but a door opening to eternity and eternal life for believers.

This is not to say that you will be happy to die. Yes, you may not want to leave your loved ones, but you will be comforted in the knowledge that you will see them again. As King David said when his baby died, "he cannot come to me, but I will go to him." You will not be able to come back to your loved ones, but as believers, they will be able to come to you.

### What Happens at the Moment of Death?

The apostle Paul explained to us that the spirit of those who die in Christ are united with the Lord "away from the body, and at home with the Lord" (2 Corinthians 5:8). Those who die without believing in Jesus go to a place of torment to await the final judgment.

## The End-Time

The sequence, descriptions, and understanding of these events continue to give rise to significant differences in their biblical interpretations. This appears to be an area we are not meant to fully understand without additional revelation or until the rapture. Nonetheless, sufficient information is given to provide us with a glimpse of what is to come. Some of the interpretations give very specific scenarios. The one I provide below, though brief, is biblical and is essentially the predominant one in the Christian community. We should probably consider these descriptions within the area of peripherals. The end-times are assured and will occur. It is just the specifics that have, to our present minds, been less than clear.

This section is compiled from the books of Daniel, Isaiah, Ezekiel, Matthew, Luke, 1 and 2 Corinthians, 1 and 2 Thessalonians, and Revelation.

### The Rapture

*Rapture* comes from the Latin *rapiemur*, which means "we will be caught up." All Bible prophecies that were to occur before the gathering up of the believers have occurred. To paraphrase the apostle Paul, when the rapture occurs, those believers who are alive will certainly not precede those who have fallen asleep but will join them with the Lord. This is not the Second Coming; it is the gathering of believers to Christ before the start of the tribulation.

### The Tribulation

Unbelievers who are still alive at the rapture will enter a seven-year period of tribulation. The first half of this period will see the coalescing of the world under one charismatic leader (believed to be the Antichrist mentioned in the Bible) who will proclaim and achieve peace throughout the land, even between the Israelis and the Arab world. He will rebuild and rule from the Jewish temple. The Jewish nation will again assume its priestly mantle and will, this time, begin to spread the gospel.

Things will get rough in the second half of the tribulation; there will be wars, pestilence, earthquakes, meteorites crashing into earth, fires, and famine. During this period, the Antichrist will turn the world against the Jews and all new Christian converts.

### The Second Coming

When all the forces of the Antichrist have gathered for Armageddon (the final and total destruction of the Jewish nation and the new converts), Jesus will make his triumphant appearance, his Second Coming, with his host of angels and believers. He will quickly destroy the armies of the Antichrist and bind Satan. With the defeat of the enemy, a period of real peace will start with Jesus in his rightful role as King.

### The Millennium

With Christ as the ruler, a thousand years of peace and tranquility will settle in throughout the world. At the end of the thousand years, Satan will be released and will initiate war against the forces of Christ. He will be defeated and permanently thrown into the lake of fire.

## Earth and Heaven

The old earth and the old heaven will be destroyed and replaced by a new heaven and new earth. There is enough information presented to indicate that there will be a heaven on earth (the new Eden) and a continuing heaven in heaven.

## The Final Judgment

Unbelievers who have died will be resurrected. Believers and unbelievers will have been separated. All unbelievers will be brought before the white throne judgment. As judgment is passed, each one will be removed to spend eternity in hell. When all the unbelievers have been judged, the believers will be called to the black throne judgment.

## The Rewards Judgment

The judging of the believers will not determine where they will spend eternity; that will have been determined the moment they believed. No, they will be judged to determine what rewards if any they will receive. It is most likely that the rewards will be predicated on the good works accomplished during their sanctification process.

## Significant Disagreements

The process and events described above come from several different books in the Bible. To a large degree, most Protestant churches subscribe to the above, while a few of these churches have some variations. The Roman Catholic Church has some distinct disagreements with a few of the eschatological events described; it believes the millennium started with the birth of Jesus and we are currently in the millennium. Catholics also believe that when people die, most will go to a place called purgatory to be purged and cleansed. When this process is completed, they will be released to go to heaven. Historically, this process could be speeded up by the support of those still living, through prayer and/or the purchase of absolutions. A further note: the concept of purgatory is extra-biblical (i.e., not in the Bible). History shows that Gregory the Great established the concept of purgatory in the late fifth century AD.

### What Will Heaven or Hell Be Like?

Having gone through separate judgments—unbelievers to hell, believers to heaven— what can we expect? As with all eschatological events, there are a few words here and there as to what they will be like. The fact that there is a heaven and a hell is explicit. What they will be like is what is not explicit. We are given one or two glimpses of them. From the few descriptive words in the Bible, heaven and hell appear to have varying degrees of intensity. The worst part of hell will be the abode of Satan and his host, closely followed by those teachers of the word who intentionally misled those who would be Christians. The less-intense part of hell will be reserved for those who did good works but did not believe in Christ.

Heaven will be ... the Bible says we (those in the flesh) do not have words to describe heaven. We must experience it to believe it! A thought races through my mind. Can you imagine your senses reaching such a heightened state of sensation that you could not only see the color red but also smell, taste, and yes, even hear it? Possible? Someday I will know.

Suffice it to say that heaven is the complete opposite of hell. The apostle Paul, in describing a believer that just made it in to heaven, said that those whose "works" do not pass the test "will be saved—even though only as one escaping through the flames" (1 Corinthians 3:15). They will arrive, probably smelling of smoke and possibly smoldering a bit, but they will arrive! They will be in the excellent part of heaven. After that, it just gets better; the more rewards you have earned, the better heaven gets.

For a heightened biblical perspective, I suggest you read the first two chapters of Genesis and the last two chapters of Revelation. Some say the Bible is encapsulated in those four chapters. There is no doubt that those four chapters are heavy hitters.

### Will God Really Send Me to Hell?

No! Skeptics often voice the opinion that they cannot accept a God that would send people to hell for all eternity just for not believing in him! It is not God who sends unbelievers to hell. When faced with a choice, believers, knowing God has a plan for everything, will petition God for guidance and will always conclude with, "Not my will but thy will be done." God honors his commitments. He gave you free will. You made your choice. With a heavy heart, he will look you in the eye and say, "Your will be done."

# Chapter 20

# Conclusion

We have covered a lot of information. We have looked at so much. My hope is that you are not overwhelmed. In writing this, my hardest struggle was to try to keep it relevant. I wanted to give you just the essentials needed to provide enough information to get you started or continue in the right direction and to give you a platform from which you could grow in God. No doubt there will be criticism that I didn't cover certain things some considered critically important. That was not my intent; my intent was merely to lay a foundation.

In the beginning of this discourse, I stated that a true religion would be able to provide answers to the three profound questions that have dogged humanity.

- Where did I come from?
- What am I doing here?
- What happens to me after I die?

As a believer, these questions practically answer themselves.

- I was created by the Almighty God
- to live for him on this earth, to help propagate his creation, to do his will, to relate with him, and
- to spend eternity with loved ones and with God after this earthly life is over.

As with the rest of this writing, this is the short answer.

Most of this endeavor was devoted to secular reasoning. I could not just tell you to start reading the Bible and to keep reading it until you understood it and agreed with its teachings. You would never have understood it without help. The apostle Paul explained, "The person without the Spirit does not accept the things from … God but considers them foolishness, and cannot understand them because they are discerned only through the Spirit" (1 Corinthians 2:14). That is why I appealed first to your intellect but then explained at the end that intellect was in and of itself not sufficient. Believing by faith was and is the only way. But now, you have been provided with secular proof and hopefully understanding that should lead you to the threshold of belief.

Attending church is always the best way to start this relationship with God. If you don't have a church, start by selecting one based on the Bible. If you're attending a church, take the time to research and study its beliefs and doctrines and compare them to the Bible.

In the event you need help finding a church, know that it is not an easy task. With the variety and number of various denominations just in the Christian religion, knowing which one is the true or the truest one can be a challenge. The most reliable measure has to be how close its doctrine and beliefs are to the Bible. If we do not use the Bible as a standard, then we have nothing but ritual and social gatherings.

People have continually tried to "improve" on scripture. Consider Jesus' many confrontations with the leaders of the church during his ministry. His most emotional episodes were with the church Pharisees, Sadducees, and Scribes. More than once, he accused them of being more concerned with their traditions and their personal privilege and power than they were of abiding with scripture and in doing God's work. They had moved away from the Bible and had instituted man's traditions in its place.

He also chastised them severely for worshipping God with their lips only, going through a lot of rituals and reciting a lot of words with no feelings from the heart.

The present religious culture is not immune to the temptation of "improving" on or altering scripture to make it more palatable. We have but to look around to see that manifestation in full display.

Not only is this an aberration of the Word of God, it also totally disregards the apostle John's warning in Revelation 22:18–19; speaking of God's words, he clearly stated, "If anyone adds anything to them, God will add to that person the plagues described … and if anyone takes words away … God will take away from that person any share in the tree of life and in the Holy City."

In the end, the only way to be sure that a particular church is adhering to biblical guidance is to take apostle Paul's advice, and after praying for guidance, to read, study, and know the Bible. Only then will you know if the ministry of that church is in keeping with God's Word.

As Christians, we should be acutely aware that while we are alive in this world, we are inexorably moving along this journey that started when we were conceived. The short period from the time we are able to understand and accept or reject the calling of Christ (age of reason) until we draw our last breath in this world is the only portion of our journey available to us in which we have the ability to decide where we will spend eternity. There are no timeouts, no do-overs, no extensions of time.

With prayer, I wish you well on your journey. Bear in mind that the decision about where you will spend the rest of eternity has to be made in this, the earthly segment of your journey. The moment you take that last breath, your final destination is set. Right now, this final destination is completely in your hands

*So where will your journey end?*

*Always be prepared to give an answer to everyone who*
*asks you to give a reason for the hope that you have.*
—1 Peter 3:15

## Review of Part 4

1. Who wrote the first five books of the Old Testament? In what approximate time period?
2. In the Council of Carthage in AD 397, church fathers canonized *in receptus* how many books that we now know as the New Testament? Explain *in receptus*.
3. What is the Apocrypha?
4. Name the three premier "witnesses" of the Bible.
5. Did Jesus ever claim to be God?
6. Define a covenant.
7. Name at least three biblical covenants.
8. What do we mean by the deity of Christ?
9. How long was the ministry of Jesus?
10. In your own words describe the gospel.
11. Name three things that give secular credence to the resurrection of Jesus.
12. In your own words describe the series of events known as the rapture, tribulation, and millennium.

# References

**Chapter 1**
*New International Version of the Bible.*
Lightfoot, Neil R., *How We Got the Bible*
Story, Dan, *Christianity on the Offense*
Story, Dan, *Defending Your Faith*

**Chapter 2**
Christian Apologetics Research Ministry, CARM.com.
Jeremiah, David, *What in the World is Going on?*

**Chapter 3**
Lightfoot, Neil R., *How We Got the Bible*
Sproul, R. C, *Can I Trust the Bible?*
Strobel, Lee, *The Case for Christ*

**Chapter 4**
*New International Version of the Bible.*
Cheney, J; S. Ellison, *Jesus Christ: The Greatest Life*,
Lewis, C. S., *Mere Christianity*,

**Chapter 5**
*New International Version of the Bible.*
CARM.org, Christia*n Apologetics Research Ministry*
Lloyd-Jones, D. Martin, *Authentic Christianity*
McKinley, Mike, *Am I Really a Christian?.*

**Chapter 6**
*New International Version of the Bible.*
CARM.org, *Christian Apologetics Research Ministry.*
New Advent, *Excerpts from Vatican I and Vatican II*

## Chapters 7–9
*New International Version of the Bible.*
Story, Dan, *Christianity on the Offense*
Story, Dan, *Defending Your Faith*
Story, Dan, *Engaging the Closed Minded*

## Chapter 10
Turk, Frank, *Cross Examined.org*
Krauss, Lawrence, *The Universe from Nothing*
Albert, David, *Quantum Mechanics*

## Chapter 11
New Advent, *Excerpts from Humanist Manifesto I and II*
Christian Apologetics Research Ministry, CARM.org.

## Chapter 12
CARM.org Christian Apologetics Research Ministry,.
Turk, Frank, *Cross Examined.org*
Dennis McCalum, *The Death of Truth,*

## Chapter 13
*New International Version of the Bible.*
Edersheim, Alfred, *Bible History: Old Testament,*
Jeremiah, David, *What in the World is Going On?.*
Jewish Virtual Library, *History of Judaism,.*
Turk, Frank, *Cross Examined.org.*

## Chapter 15
*New International Version of the Bible.*
CARM.org., *Christian Apologetics Research Ministry*
Douglas, J. D. Comfort, Philip W., Mitchel,
Donald, *Who's Who in Christian History*
Lightfoot, Neil R., *How We Got the Bible*

Mears, Henrietta C., *What the Bible is All About*
Sproul, R. C., *Can I Trust The Bible?*
Torrey, R. A., *Difficulties in the Bible*,

**Chapter 16**
*New International Version of the Bible.*
Cheney, Johnston, S. Ellisen., *Jesus Christ: The Greatest Life*,
Sproul, R. C., *What is the Trinity?*
Strobel, Lee, *The Case for Christ*,

**Chapter 17**
*New International Version of the Bible.*
Gilbert, Greg, *What is the Gospel*,
Jewish Virtual Library, *History of Judaism*,.
Utley, Bob, *The Gospel according to ...* (the series)

**Chapter 18**
*New International Version of the Bible.*
Strobel, Lee, *The Case for Christ*
Turk, Frank, *Cross Examined.org*,

**Chapter 19**
*New International Version of the Bible.*
Lloyd-Jones, D. Martin, *Authentic Christianity*
Hodges, Zane C., *Romans Deliverance from Wrath*
McKinley, Mike,. *Am I Really a Christian?*
Ryrie, Charles,. *A Survey of Bible Doctrine*,
Sproul, R. C, *Can I Be Sure I'm Saved?*.
Utley, Bob,. *Hope in Hard Times—The Final Curtain: Revelation*